One State

One State

The Only Democratic Future for Palestine-Israel

Ghada Karmi

First published 2023 by Pluto Press
New Wing, Somerset House, Strand, London WC2R 1LA
and Pluto Press, Inc.
1930 Village Center Circle, 3-834, Las Vegas, NV 89134

www.plutobooks.com

Parts of this book were first published by Pluto Press as *Married to Another Man*, 2007

British Library Cataloguing in Publication Data
A catalogue record for this book is available from the British Library

ISBN   978 0 7453 4831 5   Paperback
ISBN   978 0 7453 4832 2   PDF
ISBN   978 0 7453 4833 9   EPUB

This book is printed on paper suitable for recycling and made from fully managed and sustained forest sources. Logging, pulping and manufacturing processes are expected to conform to the environmental standards of the country of origin.

Typeset by Stanford DTP Services, Northampton, England

Simultaneously printed in the United Kingdom and United States of America

Contents

Introduction   1

1   The Problem of Zionism   8

2   Israel and the Arabs   19

3   Israel and the Jews   34

4   The Israeli-Palestinian 'Peace Process'   53

5   The One-State Solution   76

6   Eleven Days in May   151

Conclusion: The Future   161

Notes   171
Index   187

Introduction

This book is based on my previous work, *Married to Another Man*, first published in 2007. It was concerned with Israel's unresolved dilemma of how to reconcile the existence of Israel as a state for Jews with the presence of a large, non-Jewish, Palestinian population in the country. The book argued that it was an irresolvable problem, and the way forward was the creation of a shared state to include Jewish Israelis and Palestinian Arabs.

That shared state, the obstacles to its realisation, and the ways of attaining it is the focus of the present book. It is underpinned by the view that a single Palestinian-Israeli state, desirable or not, will be the inevitable outcome of Israel's action and policies over seven decades; and that Israel will fiercely reject the shared state, but will be powerless to prevent it happening.

It was always an anomaly that such an artificially constructed state as Israel ever came into existence, and was then showered with unprecedented support from powerful states – support that persists until today. It is equally anomalous that, no less than Israel itself, these same powers would rush to prevent its dissolution on any grounds. Created in the mid-twentieth century to house a people who had never been a people[1] – by the collusion of a colonial power, Britain, and a European settler movement, Zionism – Israel was established against a historical trend of mass decolonisation that ran through the second half of the twentieth century. Its violations of international law and human rights abuses are manifold, and should have disqualified it from Western support. But Israel is by no means unique in its record of abuse: other states commit similar crimes. However, such states are not usually admired or celebrated; nor do they escape censure and sanction for their actions. The Russia–Ukraine war that started in February 2022 is a case in point. It took the West no time at all to condemn Russia's illegal invasion of Ukraine, swiftly followed by the imposition of draconian economic and cultural sanctions that have crippled Russia's freedom of action ever since. By contrast, there has never been any comparable move against Israel, which illegally occupies Arab territory, regularly attacks the Palestinians living in the land it occupies, and imposes an apartheid system of rule over them.

It is 75 years since Israel was established on the ruins of Palestine. In that process, my family was forced to flee our home in Jerusalem in April 1948. The creation of Israel, officially declared one month later, marked the start of our long exile, even as our eviction was being celebrated for installing another people in our place. In the decades that followed, we watched helplessly as the new state grew in strength and dominance to become a regional superpower. Today, Israel is a nuclear state with a powerful army. It enjoys the unstinting support of Western countries, most especially the United States, which provides Israel with advanced weaponry, intelligence sharing, and political and diplomatic support. It is regarded by the West as an integral part of the Western world, and the European Union has accorded Israel a privileged status in trade and access to EU research programmes, exactly as if it were a European state.[2]

In contrast, the victims of Israel's creation, the Palestinians like me who lost out, were not honoured, commended, or given any special status. The majority of Arab states, with the notable exception of Algeria, have regarded Palestinians variously as a burden or a source of instability for their people. This attitude was explicable at one time in the historical context of the mass exodus of refugees that took place between 1947 and 1949. Palestinians, displaced by the creation of Israel on their land and at their expense, streamed out to the surrounding Arab countries. These gave the refugees a home and, in some cases such as Jordan or Syria, quasi-citizenship status, on the understanding their stay would be temporary while they awaited their return to the homeland.

That return never happened, and it was inevitable that the exiled Palestinians would go on to seek justice and fight for their rights. Many joined the radical Arab movements of the time, but eventually they formed their own liberation project, the Palestine Liberation Organisation (PLO). Unsurprisingly, such developments came to be seen as a potential threat to Arab regimes, fearful that their own populations could be radicalised in the same way.[3] The mass of ordinary Arabs throughout the region were already sympathetic to the Palestinians and supported their cause. This has remained largely the case until today. When a few Gulf States broke ranks in 2020 and signed the so-called 'Abraham Accords' with the aim of normalising relations between them and Israel, it did not negate this position. Those Israeli-Arab agreements were concluded between the governments of the United Arab Emirates, Bahrain and Israel without the permission or consultation of their Arab populations.

This divergence between the official and popular position on Palestine is mirrored in the Western world. No Western government has ever formally supported the Palestine cause, yet there is a striking level of sympathy with the Palestinians at the popular level. This is particularly marked in the US, traditionally the devoted champion of the Israeli state.[4] Even though the phenomenon is a modest one at the present time, a confluence of factors will help to enlarge it in future: activism amongst Palestinian exiles and their supporters, the use of social media, and the solidarity of Black and other radical groups. Repeated Israeli assaults on Gaza, earning ordinary

3

people's sympathy in many places, have also played their part in shoring up pro-Palestinian support.

Israel has reacted to this positive development in public support for the Palestinian cause with alarm, perhaps the best evidence for activists' growing effectiveness. Pro-Israel supporters have come up with a number of initiatives aiming to neutralise this trend. The drive to make Boycott Divestment and Sanctions (BDS) against Israel illegal in Western countries, and the ramping up of the antisemitism campaign are two examples. Both have the aim of discrediting support for Palestine as antisemitic, and hence illegitimate. As will be discussed below, these efforts have already made inroads into policy in several European counters, and especially in the US.

We must ask where this tit-for-tat situation is heading. How will Israel's denial of Palestinian rights, and Palestinian counter-resistance to it, end? After 75 years of Israel's existence, we have arrived at a point of no return for both sides in the Israeli–Palestinian conflict. Israel is entrenched in the Middle East, a powerful settler state with a commanding regional position, enjoying the benefits of a complicit and supportive Western world whatever crime it commits, and a Palestinian resistance unequal to the daunting task of changing the status quo, within a weak and disunited Arab world, part of which has already been pacified with Arab-Israeli peace treaties. As a colonial state in occupation of the totality of historic Palestine, Israel exploits all the advantages of owning the land and its resources. Having attained this favourable position, it will not willingly surrender any of its privileges in a peace agreement.

Likewise, the Palestinians will not give up either, having resisted Israel's imposition on their country in various ways: the *fedayeen* (freedom fighter) movement in the 1950s; the creation of the PLO in 1964; the conciliatory acceptance of a mini-state on 22 per cent of their original land in 1988; the two Intifadas of 1987 and 2000; the rise of Islamist resistance movements in 1989, which have fought Israel since then; the Boycott, Divestment, and Sanctions (BDS) campaign launched from inside the occupied territories in 2005, and the indefatigable activism of the Palestinian Diaspora keeping Palestine's cause alive and in the public eye.

It is obvious that no solution to the Israeli–Palestinian conflict can be envisaged in these circumstances. The two sides have irreconcilable aims, which would have to be surrendered, at least in part, to make a peace deal possible. That hope of compromise has been the basis of the Israeli-Palestinian negotiations since 1993, which have now ended in failure. The reality, persistently ignored because it is inconvenient for the parties pushing for a negotiated settlement, is that Israel is not interested in changing a status quo which satisfies all its requirements, and hence would be unwilling to consider any settlement that entails even a minimal surrender of its gains. Since Israel is the stronger party, and no one is willing to put pressure on Israel, that inevitably leaves the Palestinians to compromise by whittling down their demands to a point which Israel might accept. But that would mean a surrender of their most basic rights, which they cannot accept either.

If ordinary Israelis were asked how they would like to see the conflict end, they would almost certainly wish for a magical disappearance of the Palestinians in their midst. And if ordinary Palestinians were asked the same question they would wish to put back the clock to a time before Israel's creation, when Palestine was their undisputed country. Neither wish can be granted, and the reality is that two communities live in the same land and need a civilised way of sharing it.

That has been the main driver of the campaigns for the 'one-state solution' which have appeared in the last two decades. But egalitarian and moral as this aim seems, we cannot ignore the fact that it is a solution neither side wants. Israelis will not accept Palestinians as equal partners in a country they are accustomed to regarding as exclusively their own. Palestinians, with lifelong experiences of Israelis as usurpers and aggressors, will find living with them as equal citizens hard to stomach.

In neither case can the one-state solution, however democratic, be said to solve the problem for these two peoples. The fact that small groups of peace-loving, principled individuals and their supporters from both sides are working diligently together towards a one-state solution does not alter this reality. For the mass of Jewish Israelis and Palestinian Arabs, the antipathy on both sides is real and a serious obstacle to coexistence.

Yet, a shared state is the only way this impasse will end – not because it is wanted by either side, but because it is inevitable. It is the contention of this book that the logic of the situation before us must lead to the formation of one democratic state in place of the current ethnocentric, apartheid state of Israel. It will not happen solely as a result of one-state campaigns and solidarity movements – although they will help – but rather through people's natural resistance to relentless oppression leading to the ultimate overthrow of their oppressors. Like all brutal regimes, Israel will fight ferociously to keep the status quo, and it is an irony that it was the Israelis' obdurate, short-sighted and avaricious tactics over the years that will lead inexorably to this result: an outcome Israel never sought, one that would spell the end of Zionism and bring the whole Israeli project to an end.

In what follows, we will examine this process and how it came about despite the unique support, not just for Israel, but for the *idea* of Israel. And how, at the same time, and despite their reluctance, the one-state end point is the only way Palestinians can regain their usurped rights. We will analyse the nature of Israel's state ideology, Zionism; the effect of Israel's creation on the Arab world in which it is situated; the hold

Israel has on Jews; the attempts to make peace between Israel and the Palestinians, and conclude with an account of the one-democratic-state initiatives, past and present.

At the time of writing, none of these had become a reality, but the reader should be in no doubt that the one democratic state is the destination for both peoples. Before it happens, there will be more struggle and suffering as Palestinians fight against increasing Israeli oppression and expulsion, tacitly and overtly supported by Western inaction, and collusion amongst pro-Western Arab states. But the greater Israel's suppression of Palestinian rights, the quicker the end point will be reached.

Israel was created and maintained against the logic of history; and the same historical logic will dictate its inevitable ending.

CHAPTER ONE

The Problem
of Zionism

At the outset of this book, it is important to frame the situation in Israel/Palestine within its proper context. Israel is not a natural phenomenon in the Middle East, did not arise as a normal result of circumstance, and had no historical antecedents in the region, despite the biblical mythology employed to suggest the contrary. It is a settler colonial state, set up *de novo*, aiming to provide a home for the Jews of the world, or as many of them as would come, with the aim of maintaining a permanent Jewish majority presence in that state.

When the Zionists resolved in 1897 to establish a Jewish state in Palestine, they were aware that it was already home to an indigenous non-Jewish population. How then now to create and maintain a state for another people in a land already inhabited? Squaring that circle has been the essence of Israel's dilemma ever since its establishment and the cause of the Palestinian tragedy that it led to. It could not have been otherwise, for what the Zionists envisaged was a project that was bizarre and, on the face of it, unworkable: namely to set up an ethnically -defined, Jews-only collective, existing on a land belonging to another people and to their exclusion. Moreover, this new creation was supposed to prosper in perpetuity, irrespective of native opposition.

It was inevitable that a project necessitating the appropriation of a land already inhabited by a people defined as ethnically unacceptable could only have been realised by a mixture of violence and coercion. To have any hope of long-term success, the new state thus created would have to maintain itself through constant military superiority and powerful backing by its sponsor, the West. The corollary to this was that the Arabs would have to remain too weak and disunited to offer much resistance, with the calculation that Israel's powerful army would swiftly despatch any resistance that arose.

This, in substance, is the Zionist project, whose main aims came to be realised in the creation of Israel in 1948, but which was never able to resolve the problem of the Palestinians. Its dilemma has nowhere been better expressed than by the Israeli historian, Benny Morris, in an interview with the Israeli daily, *Haaretz*, on 8 January 2004.[1] In a lucid exposé of classical Zionist thinking which merits quotation at length, he encapsulates all of Zionism's major elements, its inherent implausibility as a practical project, its arrogance, racism and self-righteousness, and the insurmountable obstacle to it of Palestine's original population, which refuses to go away. The conditions that must pertain for the Jewish state's creation and survival required the expulsion of much of the indigenous population and the need to maintain Israeli supremacy in the face of the inevitable Arab hostility. As Morris says:

A Jewish state would not have come into being without the uprooting of 700,000 Palestinians. Therefore it was necessary to uproot them. There was no choice but to expel that population. If the desire to establish a Jewish state here is legitimate, there was no other choice … The need to establish this state in this place overcame the injustice that was done to the Palestinians by uprooting them.

It follows that the future survival of Israel may necessitate further Palestinian population 'transfers'. Morris maintains the mistake the Zionists made was to have allowed any Palestinians to remain:

> If the end of the story turns out to be a gloomy one for the Jews, it will be because Ben-Gurion [Israel's first prime minister] did not complete the transfer in 1948. Because he left a large and volatile demographic reserve in the West Bank and Gaza and within Israel itself ... In other circumstances, apocalyptic ones, which are liable to be realized in five or ten years, I can see expulsions. If we find ourselves ... in a situation of warfare ... acts of expulsion will be entirely reasonable. They may even be essential ... if the threat to Israel is existential, expulsion will be justified.

Inevitably, Zionism resulted in the creation of hostility amongst its victims, since the displaced Palestinians have never been reconciled to the Zionist project and 'can't tolerate the existence of a Jewish state'. Given this, Zionism could only have succeeded by the use of superior force: 'There is not going to be peace in the present generation. There will not be a solution. We are doomed to live by the sword.' He recognises that Zionism had unrealistic expectations:

> The whole Zionist project is apocalyptic. It exists within hostile surroundings and in a certain sense its existence is unreasonable. It wasn't reasonable for it to succeed in 1881 and it wasn't reasonable for it to succeed in 1948 and it's not reasonable that it will succeed now.

In the final analysis, Morris concludes the Zionist project is faced with two options: perpetual cruelty and repression of others, or the end of the dream. For Zionists, the latter is tragically unthinkable.

Following this interview, liberal Israelis attacked Morris for what they viewed as his right-wing views. Yet, he should have been commended for his candour and honesty in articulating what most Zionists feel but do not say. In these extracts, he accurately reflects the anxieties and soul-searching that beset Zionism as the Jewish state enters seven decades of its existence.

The problem was also clear to Zionism's earliest leaders. One of the most important of these, Vladimir (later, Ze'ev) Jabotinsky, put it well in 1923 in an article entitled 'The Iron Wall'.

'Every indigenous people', he wrote about the Palestinian Arabs' expected reaction to the Zionist project, 'will resist alien settlers as long as they see any hope of ridding themselves of the danger of foreign settlement.' A 'voluntary' agreement with the Palestinians was thus impossible. He ridiculed his fellow Zionists who thought such an agreement was a necessary condition of Zionism by saying that they might as well abandon the project. The alternative he advocated was for Zionist colonisation to develop 'under the protection of a force independent of the local population – an iron wall which the native population cannot break through.'[2] (The iron wall refers to a wall of bayonets.)

Moshe Dayan, Israel's chief of staff many years later, reiterates these same ideas in a different way. Speaking in 1956 at the funeral of a young Israeli killed by an Arab 'infiltrator' near the Egyptian frontier, he said:

> Let us not today fling accusations at the murderers. Who are we that we should argue against their hatred? For eight years now, they sit in their refugee camps in Gaza and, before their very eyes we turn into our homestead the land and the villages in which they and their forefathers have lived. We are a generation of settlers, and without the steel

helmet and the cannon we cannot plant a tree and build a home. Let us not shrink back when we see the hatred fermenting and filling the lives of hundreds of thousands of Arabs, who sit all around us. Let us not avert our gaze, so that our hand shall not slip. This is the fate of our generation, the choice of our life – to be prepared and armed, strong and tough – or otherwise, the sword will slip from our fist, and our life will be snuffed out.[3]

If Dayan had had foresight, he might have added that it was not just his generation but also all subsequent Israeli generations who would have to continue this tough stance or else have their lives 'snuffed out'. For the central issue confronting Israel has always been how to stem the tide of opposition to its existence.

Inevitably, Arabs saw Israel as an alien body implanted in the heart of their region. They rejected it, just as the human body rejects a foreign organ graft. In such cases, doctors strive hard to suppress the body's rejection to save the patient's life, and this noble aim is generally taken to justify the medical effort and expense entailed in achieving it. Zionism sees its own struggle in similar terms: to fulfil an aim no less noble, that of maintaining a Jewish state as a solution to the long-standing persecution of Jews. In the furtherance of what is perceived as a self-evidently moral project, measures normally deemed to be unacceptable become tolerable as a means to an end which no one could disagree with. And it is this which makes Zionism such a dangerous ideology. The conviction of moral rightness that lies at its heart has engaged most Jews, and a substantial number of non-Jews, in the liberal West. Shortly after issuing his famous Declaration, Arthur Balfour expressed it long ago in this way: 'Zionism, be it right or wrong, good or bad, is rooted in age-long traditions, in present deeds, in future hopes, of far profounder import than the desires and prejudices of the 700,000 Arabs who now inhabit that ancient land.'[4]

That was in 1917. In the ensuing three decades, the Nazi Holocaust had completed the task of persuading Zionism's Western sponsors that a haven for persecuted Jews was an imperative. And few people in the West have ever seriously disagreed with this proposition since then. It is inextricably bound up with the general perception of Palestine as the rightful and necessary home of the Jews, a view that runs very deep within the hearts and minds of many Jews, however liberal, and a majority of others in the West. To challenge this concept, to argue that the Jews (or any other foreign group) had no right whatsoever to Palestine as a *state* and, no matter what their sufferings, were not justified in dispossessing its people, is tantamount to sacrilege. The campaign to equate anti-Israel criticism with antisemitism, shrewdly instigated by the Zionists and vigorously pursued today, has compounded this situation. Add to this the fact that a linkage between Jews and the Holy Land already existed in the minds of Western Christians, whether practising or not, and the case for Israel seems unassailable.

Truly, for the Palestinians, who were the chief victims of the enterprise, to take on this mixture of received wisdom, psychology, emotion and entrenched beliefs is a monumental task. Their case has been so effectively subsumed in the dominant Israeli narrative that, for years, they were not expected even to question or resist it. They and the rest of the Arab world were supposed to share everyone else's view of Israel as a moral project and not to object to its creation. Hence, Arab hostility to Israel appears mysterious or just spiteful, and it has only been since the First and Second Palestinian Intifadas in 1987 and 2000, respectively, and the repeated assaults on Gaza with the brutality of Israel's occupation exposed, that Palestinians have been legitimately permitted to object. The parameters of these objections, however, are strictly limited by an implicit consensus on what Palestinians can legitimately hope for: that Israel may be expected to ease its occupation and that the end of the process can be a Palestinian state of sorts in the post-1967 territories. The latter is regarded as the pinnacle of Palestinian ambition, with any claim to the land that was lost to Israel before 1967 totally excluded from the equation, as if there had been no Palestinian history before 1967 and Israel had always been a natural part of the landscape.

Such a scenario may be superficially convincing, even comforting, for Israel and the West. It implies that Palestinians can delete the past and their own grievances, that they can be content with a small portion of their original homeland and that the refugees and other displaced people who are currently lodging in various countries will altruistically and unilaterally give up on their hopes of repatriation. It is only possible to think in this way if one entirely disregards the feelings and reactions of the people in whose midst the Jewish state was established. This essentially colonialist and racist thinking imbued the Balfour Declaration,[5] which gave the impetus to the whole process. The idea that a foreign people could be invited into another land without the knowledge or permission of the native population would now be regarded as outrageous. But it still informs the Western approach to the Arabs in this conflict. And under the weight of this pervasive view, some Arabs have begun to doubt themselves, to feel that their rejection of Israel is somehow unfeeling and ungracious.

After over seven decades of Israeli nationhood, maintained through superior power and ceaseless Western support, a change in the Arab position vis-à-vis Israel is clearly discernible. Matters have moved on significantly since the days of Gamal Abdel Nasser, Egypt's president until 1970, and the refusal of Arab states to recognise or deal with Israel. Today, there are peace plans that extend recognition and full acceptance to Israel as a normal part of the region, of which the 2002 Saudi peace plan is the best example. Though it was never implemented, normalisation of relations with Israel is proceeding apace at the formal and informal level. In 2020, the United Arab Emirates, Bahrain, Morocco and Sudan normalised relations with Israel. Normalisation, viewed by the West as a reasonable response to Israel's existence in the region, is in fact no such thing.

When one considers what the Arabs were required to do in this process – to host an alien people who carved out a state for themselves on Arab land, and did so, moreover, with a Western support that was callously indifferent to the effects of this enterprise on those at the receiving end – it is not reasonable. And more so when they were expected to accept Israel without questioning the Israeli project's basic tenet: that there had to be a Jewish state in Palestine *as of right*. That Jewish/Western imperative was supposed to justify *to Arabs* every excess and every abuse that Israel meted out to them in the last seven decades. That, despite this monstrous imposition, the Arabs allowed the Zionist project to flourish, might suggest to many that it has finally succeeded.

But has it? The Palestinians are still there – damaged, fragmented, occupied and oppressed, to be sure – but still there, both physically and politically, and in fact more than ever before. Seven decades of Israeli effort to destroy them and resolve the original Zionist dilemma have not succeeded. They still constitute an obstacle to Zionism that refuses to go away. There is still no peace agreement to end the conflict and Israel's supremacy in arms and technology, its powerful friends and devoted supporters have not bought it a normal, peaceful existence. The Jewish state is not a haven for Jews seeking refuge. It is more dangerous and unstable than anywhere else where Jews now reside, constantly under threat and unsure of its long-term future. Putting up the barricades against 'terrorism' and the Arab 'demographic threat' cannot dam the tide forever, and the attempt has converted Israel into a quasi-fascist state, embarrassing to its supporters and unloved by nearly everyone else.

As the people living in Israel continue to elaborate a new 'Israeli' identity, they will become ever more disconnected from the Jews outside Israel, to whom already many of them appear alien.[6] Jewish immigration into Israel is increasingly difficult, as it fails to attract more diaspora Jews to emigrate. The desperation to ward off the inevitable is discernible in previous hunts for 'Jews' in Africa, Peru, India and elsewhere,[7] and the numbers of non-Jewish immigrants admitted to Israel as Jews (for example, thousands of Soviet immigrants are reported to be Christians).[8]

The damage, dislocation and suffering which the Palestinians and Arabs of the region have been forced to endure in order to make the Zionist experiment succeed – even in the cause of solving the problem of Jewish persecution in Europe – are far in excess of what could reasonably have been demanded from any group of people. It was particularly deleterious to the Arabs in the first half of the twentieth century when Zionism was taking root, emerging as they were from long-term Ottoman rule to be dominated again almost at once by the Western powers. As such, they were singularly ill-equipped to protect themselves effectively against the Zionist intrusion. In many ways, they remain so today, owing in no small measure to the existence of Israel in their midst. The conflict thus generated was inevitable and entirely predictable. To date, all attempts to end it have failed.

The central cause for this failure is the Zionist imperative to create and maintain a Jewish majority in a land belonging to non-Jews. The obsessive adherence to this imperative has led to a variety of Israeli initiatives, all of which aimed to minimise the Palestinian presence in the country and ensure that it did not re-emerge. Hence, a series of plans, combining expulsion (as happened in 1948 and 1967 and continues at a slower pace today) and territorial partition heavily in favour of the Jewish state were devised. This is a difficult task in a land the size of Wales, whose natural resources are scattered throughout. Trying to apportion these on a basis of inequitable sharing in a partitioned land has proved complicated and unworkable except as outright theft. No formulation has appeared so far that can satisfy Israeli demands and ensure Palestinian acquiescence in such a deal.

Nor can there ever be, for the 'peace' proposals are all flawed by injustice and gross inequality. Such deals may be imposed by the stronger party on the weaker one and may succeed for a while, but they will not last. A durable solution must address the issue of justice and, for Palestinians, so traduced in this conflict, that will mean affording them – all those inside and outside Palestine – a future life in dignity and equality in their homeland. As one of the Palestinians 'outside', the issue of justice is paramount in my thinking. The fact that I do not live under Israeli occupation, nor in a refugee camp, nor as an unequal Arab citizen of Israel, makes no difference to this position. All of us who grew up in the West were exposed to Western assumptions about the 'rightness' of Israel's creation and the careless dismissal of what that enterprise had meant for the natives of the country.

The two-state solution was touted for years as the answer to the problem, including by many Palestinians for their own reasons. Yet, how fair was it to the indigenous people of Palestine, most of whom had been displaced outside it in camps or in foreign countries, that their land should be unequally sliced, with the lion's share going to the invader? Why should they have been expected to accept solutions that took no account of the reality of their situation? It is clear that, had the two-state solution as proposed come into being, the majority of Palestinians (who live in the Diaspora) would have been excluded. What would happen to these people? To solve their problem, Israel and its Western allies have come up with a hotchpotch of proposals, partition for some, emigration for others and compensation for yet others – untidy solutions that can only cause further dislocation and hardship and compound the initial injustice. No peace agreement can last under these conditions.

Justice also requires that the Israeli Jewish community now living in that new homeland – and no matter how it got there – be similarly entitled to dignity and equality. In the chapters that ensue, I will argue that the only possible solution that can provide these twin imperatives will be that of a single state in an unpartitioned land where both peoples may live together. There is no other sensible way to accommodate their needs and, had it not been for Israel's destructive and foolish pursuit of an ethnic state for Jews alone, the one-state solution would have been implemented long ago.

CHAPTER TWO

Israel and the Arabs

The profound damage done to the Arab world by the creation of Israel is a major, untold story in the West. For the Arabs, Israel's presence in their midst has quite simply been an unmitigated disaster. This may come as a surprise to many Western readers, encouraged over decades to regard Israel as a natural part of the Middle Eastern landscape, potentially beneficial to a backward region, and to disregard in equal measure what Arabs might feel about it. Yet, an understanding of Israel's impact on the Arab world was always crucial to the search for a resolution to the conflict.

In 1948, the Arabs found themselves confronted with a new creation, Israel, which was alien to them in every sense. Its governing ethos was European and the bulk of its population was also European. (The 'Arab' Jews, who augmented the existing Palestinian Jewish community, came later, but were subsumed into the ruling Western structure, at least at the beginning.[1]) As such, Arabs could neither understand it nor deal with it. The year 1948 was immensely traumatic for the Arabs. Not only were they powerless to prevent Israel's creation, but they also failed to defeat it in the war that immediately ensued. Their ill-trained, smaller armies, prevented by the colonial powers which still dominated them from being useful for anything more than a security role at home, stood little chance against the highly motivated, trained and better equipped Jewish forces. They were impotent to protect the Palestinians from dispossession, something that at the time shocked and appalled every Arab who watched it happen, and just as impotent to halt Israel's expansion and growing power in the region.

From the beginning, Israel enjoyed enormous support from the major Western powers, as we have noted, which crucially enabled the Zionist project to 'bed down' in a hostile and alien region. Few people, blinded as most Westerners were by widespread projections of Israel's helplessness and vulnerability, realised how extensive and generous that support was, and how, without it, the Zionist experiment might have ended before it began.

The Arab world paid a heavy price for the success of that experiment, which must rate as the single most cataclysmic event to hit the Middle East region since the First World War. While the front-line states of Egypt, Jordan, Syria and Lebanon were the most affected, the consequences of Israel's presence have reverberated throughout the region. No other conflict has lasted as long as that consequent on Israel's creation. There has not been a single decade since then when Israel has not been in combat with its neighbours. This has damaged the political process in the Arab world, which has come to look to and depend on its army generals for leadership and to admire military strength and violence. The Arab Human Development Report prepared for the UN Development Programme (UNDP) in 2002, revealed the extent of the Arab world's retardation in several key areas. It concluded that the Israeli occupation cast a pall over the region's entire political and economic life, posed a threat to all Arab countries, and that the Arab–Israeli conflict was 'a major impediment to human development in the region'.[2]

The Arabs were forced to respond to the creation of Israel in various ways, all of them deleterious. Militarisation was top of this list. Struggling with post-independence at the time of Israel's establishment, the Arab states should have been focused on their own political and social development.

The front-line states were instead dragged into wars, which diverted their resources into armaments and surveillance, even more than they were already spending on other threats. Since they did not win the wars with Israel (the 1973 war is seen by Arabs as a possible exception), they were set back each time, with loss of territory or a failure to regain all of it – as in the 1973 war – and a need to rearm even more extravagantly than before. This arms build-up was aggravated by the willingness of the major weapons-exporting states – the United States, the former Soviet Union, France and Britain – to sell arms to the region. The Middle East is the biggest per capita spender on arms in the developing world. Arab military spending in the late 1990s accounted for 7.4 per cent of GNP, three times the world average of 2.4 per cent. In 2020, the World Bank estimated military expenditure in Jordan to be 5.0 per cent of GDP, and in Lebanon 3.0 per cent, as compared to US expenditure of 3.7 per cent in the same year. The average for the Arab world was 5.7 per cent, contrasted with the world average of 2.2 per cent in 2021.

Israel's presence in the region encouraged the factionalisation of the Arab world along ethnic and religious lines. Ben-Gurion during the 1950s had propounded a vision of a reorganised Middle East wherein Jordan would be divided into an east bank extending to Iraq (and used to house the Palestinian refugees) and a west bank being joined to Israel. Lebanon would be split into a Muslim south annexed to Israel, while the rest would become a Maronite Christian entity, allied to the Jewish state.

Lebanon was severely destabilised by years of Israeli occupation and interference, its fragile confessional system of government repeatedly under stress. Israel's protracted occupation of southern Lebanon (1982–2000) left indelible scars on the economic and social life of the local community. Israel's support of minorities elsewhere in the Arab world, and penetration of ruling circles with bribes and inducements, has been instrumental in causing the enormous disruption that the Arab region is witnessing today. For example, Israel cultivated relations with Iraqi Kurds for many years, aiming to weaken Iraq's government;[3] it has played the same role with regard to Sudan by forging ties with Southern Sudan.[4] Nor should one be surprised that Israel chose such a strategy. It was the logical way to weaken its enemies and strengthen its position in the region.

Israel's policy of making separate deals with individual Arab states, so as to split Arab ranks, was another divisive strategy aiming to break up their resistance. A variety of diplomatic arrangements between Israel and the Arab states were actively pursued towards that end. Egypt, the PLO and Jordan concluded formal agreements with the Jewish state in 1979, 1993 and 1994 respectively. In 2020, normalisation of relations has been effected with the United Arab Emirates, Bahrain, Morocco and Sudan. In addition, contacts at lower levels have been made in the last decade with Tunisia, Mauritania and Qatar. Saudi ministers, including to the Crown Prince Muhammad bin Sultan, have been reported to be meeting with their Israeli counterparts. As far back as 2005, Silvan Shalom, Israel's foreign minister at the time, boasted openly that ten Arab states would be establishing relations with the Jewish state before long.[5]

Despite these new alliances, it needs to be remembered that Israeli strategy from the 1950s onwards aimed at creating a network of non-Muslim, non-Arab countries linked to Israel and especially those states opposed to pan-Arabism and Islam as a unifying factor. In addition, Israel sought to neutralise or win over those non-Arab states which supported the Arab cause. Hence, it cultivated clandestine contacts with pre-Khomeini Iran, established ties with Turkey, Ethiopia and the Christian south of Sudan, aiming to surround the Arab world with a ring of antipathetic states. This policy of encirclement became more overt over time, and resulted in a close liaison with Turkey, despite tensions following the US/British invasion of Iraq.[6] The Israeli presence in Ethiopia expanded to include a series of educational and development projects, and in 2004, following the Ethiopian foreign minister's visit to Israel, both countries signed an agreement to enhance cultural, educational and scientific cooperation. Israel's mission in Addis Ababa is the largest after that of the US.

Neighbouring Eritrea also became the recipient of intense Israeli attention. In line with Israel's policy of breaking up all Arab or pro-Arab networks and creating enmity towards them, Israel sought from the 1960s onwards to 'de-Arabise' the Horn of Africa by exerting its own influence there, an enterprise in which it seems to have signally succeeded.[7] After decades of assistance to Ethiopia in its war against Eritrea, Israel succeeded in reversing Eritrean hostility towards it. An Israeli embassy was opened in Asmara, in 1991, to which the Eritreans eventually responded by opening their own embassy in Israel in 2003. This reversal in the Eritrean position, traditionally a sympathetic one to the Arabs (as was theirs towards Eritrea), and given Israel's long-standing support for the Ethiopians against Eritrea, must be counted among Israel's more remarkable diplomatic achievements.

The same policy of encirclement and neutralisation of pro-Arab states underlay Israel's latterly cultivated relations with India, which until 1992 had taken a staunchly pro-Palestinian position and had no diplomatic ties with the Jewish state. Since the new détente under the Bharatiya Janata Party, which came into power in 1998 in a coalition that ruled until 2004 and resumed in 2014, trade between the two has increased and a close security relationship has developed, with intelligence sharing and joint military exercises, threatening India's neighbouring Muslim state, Pakistan. Consequently, the latter began to reconsider its traditionally hostile stance towards Israel.

The threat that Israel posed to the Arab world has meant that generations of young Arabs were reared on an unhealthy diet of enmity and confrontationalism. Instead of looking to a normal, secure future in which to develop their and their countries' potential, they were instead focused on hostility, and this led to the growth of an array of radical non-state groups and movements opposing Israel and its backers. This is especially true among Palestinians. From 1994, Islamist groups began to carry out acts of violence never seen before in Palestinian society, which had traditionally been secular and peaceable. Though Israel was not responsible for the initial establishment of a branch of the Muslim Brotherhood in Palestine in the 1940s, the later growth of Palestinian Islamic fundamentalism can be traced back to Israel's tacit encouragement after the 1967 occupation of the Palestinian territories. By turning a blind eye to the growth of these movements, which established a considerable network of welfare services in Gaza and the West Bank, it allowed them to become fully established and also armed. Israel's aim in supporting the Islamist groups was to use them as a counterforce to the overwhelmingly (secular) nationalist PLO.[8]

Hamas, formally created out of the Palestine Muslim Brotherhood in 1987, is a case in point. Initially encouraged and helped to develop with Israel's support in order to undermine the PLO (a ploy which failed), it turned to opposing Israel instead during the First Intifada.[9] Its aim to establish an Islamic state in the whole of Palestine, which it regards as an Islamic *waqf* (land belonging to the Muslims in perpetuity), though not a concept invented by Hamas, may be seen as the mirror image to *Eretz Israel* (the land of Israel). This phrase refers to the Jewish idea that the land must be held as the patrimony of the Jewish people, and the whole of it must form the

Jewish state. Nevertheless, most Palestinians were not fundamentalists and Palestinian society was generally lukewarm in its response to the Islamists. Support for these groups usually ran at some 10 to 20 per cent on the West Bank and 30 per cent at most in Gaza.

It was only since the start of the Second Intifada and the failure of the 1993 Oslo Agreement, and with it the collapse of secular resistance, that Islamists have enjoyed increased support for their uncompromising opposition to Israel. This phenomenon accounts for the decisive election of Hamas in the Palestinian Legislative Council elections in early 2006. Aware of the secular nature of Palestinian society, the new leadership was at pains to maintain that it would not impose Islamic rule on the people.

The phenomenon of suicide bombing, not confined to Islamic groups, was a late and particularly ugly manifestation of Palestinian reaction to Israel. Its routine condemnation by Israeli and Western observers was neither enlightening nor effective, and only served to obscure its true origins and explanation. Its Islamic colouration arose within a broader regional context in which Arab nationalism, weakened by decades of Western onslaught on behalf of Israel, gave way to religion as the primary intellectual motivation.[10] It is sobering to realise that by 2006, literally scores of young Palestinians, who should have wanted to embrace life, were on the contrary eager to kill themselves in order to damage Israeli society. That a traditionally peaceable, agrarian and family-centred people should have come to accept the sacrifice of their young men and women in the struggle against Israel was an eloquent and horrific testament to the way in which they were damaged by it. It is this that should have engaged the minds of Western politicians and prompted them to address the cause, which did not stop at the Palestinians only.

25

For, through the narrow prism of their preoccupations, these desperate young people were expressing their rejection of something all other Arabs rejected as well: the fact that they were made to host a state which ensured a continued hegemonic Western presence in their region – since Israel, as we saw, could never have been established nor survived except with Western support. It had stolen their land and resources, and had schemed ceaselessly to control them, had wooed their enemies, and worked against their interests in every field, from the use of water to their hopes of political unity. And it posed an ever-present military threat through its massive arsenal, including nuclear weapons.

The deleterious effects of Israel's establishment on Palestinian soil are well documented. The cardinal factor, which set the Palestinians on a tragic and downward course, was their dispossession. Between 1947 and 1949, most Palestinians lost their homes.[11] This terrible event ensued a protracted indigenous struggle that started in the early 1920s against the Zionists and the British, who ruled the country through the Mandate, during which Palestinian hopes for independence were crushed and subordinated to the needs of the incoming Jews. Some early Zionists, perhaps foreseeing some of this, imagined a different scenario for Jews and Arabs in Palestine. They included such figures as Judah Magnes, the Hebrew University's first president, Martin Buber and Arthur Ruppin, all of whom represented a small Zionist minority which saw Arab-Jewish coexistence as possible and desirable.[12] They established Brit Shalom in the 1930s, an organisation devoted to these ideas.

They envisaged a shared state between Jews and Arabs, and were interested in unification between the Arab states, in which the Jews could become a component. Some of this group did not want a Jewish state at all, but rather the freedom to express their culture. David Ben-Gurion himself put forward a plan in

1934 for a union of Arab states to which the Palestinians could be linked, allowing for a Jewish majority to develop in Palestine without conflict (and become a state, though he did not communicate this to his Palestinian interlocutors).[13]

But the majority Zionist drive towards statehood (in which Ben-Gurion became a prominent leader) overtook these attempts at accommodation and coexistence. Long before the UN Partition Resolution was passed in 1947 (which the Zionists eagerly accepted),[14] Ben-Gurion was clear on his ultimate goal of a Jewish state to replace Palestine. In 1937, he wrote in a letter, 'Erect a Jewish state at once, even if it is not in the whole land. The rest will come in the course of time. It must come.'[15] It is tempting to speculate how differently things might have turned out had it been the Brit Shalom faction and not Ben-Gurion's that succeeded.

The 1948 *Nakba*, or catastrophe, did more than dispossess the Palestinians. It destroyed their whole society and led to their fragmentation and dispersal. Today, they live as disparate communities, some 5 million in refugee camps; 1.8 million as Israeli citizens in Israel; approximately 6 million in the West Bank and Gaza under Israeli occupation (2021 figures); and an estimated 3–5 million as exiles in a variety of countries around the world.[16] Altogether, over 10 million Palestinians were sacrificed in order to accommodate 7 million Jews, most of them until recently from distant countries. From 1964 until 1993, the Palestinians managed a sort of unity under the umbrella of the PLO, which enabled them to feel a sense of cohesion. But after the signing of the Oslo Accords in 1993 and the return of Yasser Arafat and most of the Palestinian leadership to Palestinian territory in 1994, the PLO was effectively marginalised and, by 2005, existed in barely more than name.[17] This left millions of exiled Palestinians leaderless and fragmented once again. At the same time, those who lived under Israeli occupation experienced daily privation and hardship on a scale unimaginable to most people. So often repeated was this fact, that it became almost banal, and people were virtually inured to the daily reports of Palestinian suffering, however horrifying.

Thus, the creation of Israel converted a settled, mostly agricultural society into a nation of refugees, exiles, second-class citizens and communities under military occupation. From 1948 onwards, every attempt was made to erase all traces of the Arab presence in the new Israel so as to destroy the Arab character and distinctive history of the old Palestine. Place names were changed from Arabic to Hebrew as a deliberate policy instituted in 1949 by Ben-Gurion, which aimed to find ancient or Biblical equivalents for the Palestinian towns and villages and produce a 'Hebrew map' of Palestine.[18] The same policy continued after 1967 with the renaming of Muslim and Christian sites in the Old City of Jerusalem.[19] Buildings and villages were demolished, and in their place new European-style structures and settlements sprang up. So effective was this erasure that the locations of many of the old villages are scarcely recognisable, and it has become the task of Palestinian historians like Walid Khalidi and the researcher, Salman Abu Sitta, to try and re-map them.[20] More recently, settlements built directly above Palestinian villages use the village names with the addition of the Hebrew word for 'upper', and often the Arabic has been distorted to make it unrecognisable as such. In time, it may be difficult to remember which of the two had been the original, and the Palestinian village will have been in effect effaced.

The Israeli campaign against the Palestinians was a system-atic assault on the collective memory, identity and cohesion of a whole society that aimed to extirpate the idea that anything coherent and non-Jewish had pre-dated Israel. The damage this has done to the Palestinians in physical, social and psycho-logical terms is incalculable and has yet to be fully assessed.

In the early years of the state, for example, Israel instituted a policy deliberately aimed at destroying the cohesion of Palestinian society. Israeli agents secretly incited conflict amongst Palestinians, arming and otherwise favouring certain groups amongst them, and devising ways to prevent the emergence of a Palestinian educated class and the formation of a Palestinian leadership.[21] Ongoing oral history projects have tried to document the 1948 experiences and their consequences, since few written records were made of this tragic story.[22]

The Arab response to Israel's existence has wavered between war and appeasement. From the start, there were only two theoretical options before them: either to dismantle Israel (as a *state*) or to accommodate it in some way. Going down the first route had clearly failed, and could never have succeeded, given Arab military weakness and disunity of purpose, Arab dependence on Western powers and the latter's determination to prevent Israel's destruction. Apart from a brief demonstration of Arab military and economic power when during the 1973 October War an oil embargo had been imposed by the Gulf States, there had been no effective use of Arab power against Israel. On the contrary, Arab regimes fought each other (Egypt's futile war in Yemen, the Syrian conflict with Iraq, Iraq's invasion of Kuwait, for example) and weakened their position vis-à-vis Israel.

That left the second option, which entailed a range of possibilities. At one end was full, unresisting acceptance of Israel and all it did. This could never have been acceptable to Arab populations, even if Arab leaders had felt differently. And at the other were compromise arrangements of various kinds: non-belligerency treaties, negotiations over borders and resources, and a resolution of the Palestinian problem including the refugees, leading to full diplomatic recognition and normalisation of relations. For this option to succeed, it required a readiness on the part of Israel, no less than that of the Arabs, to do the same. It would also have required that Israel view itself as a Middle Eastern state, not just *in* the region, but *of* it.

In the event, we had the worst of all outcomes. The Arabs did not succeed in defeating Israel, nor did any of their efforts at peaceful accommodation work. Surrendering to Israel through peace treaties has not removed widespread popular hostility towards it, or prevented Israel from oppressing the Palestinians. The region is unstable largely as a result of Israeli-Western interference, and Israel's stance against Iran has added another dangerous dimension to the mix with incalculable consequences.

The heart of the problem meanwhile remained what it always was: the conflict between Israel and the Palestinians, with the additional complication that the world assumed it was up to the Arabs to solve it. This unjust imposition, resented by Arabs, needs to be borne in mind when assessing their performance in this regard. The fact that Israel continued to abuse the Palestinians and deprive them of their basic rights set a limit on how far the Arab states could respectably go down the route of accommodation. Although in 2020 this limit was breached by several normalisation agreements between Israel and some Gulf states, Morocco and Sudan, these were concluded between governments, not peoples.

One Palestinian right in particular, the right of return for refugees, presented a special problem for the Arab states. For 75 years, Israel had been able to evade its responsibility for creating the refugee problem and for its resolution. It was the front-line Arab states, instead, that bore the brunt of Palestinian displacement, sometimes at great cost to their own economy and stability.

Lebanon is a case in point, where the Palestinian refugee camps had engendered a guerrilla movement that gave rise to cross-border attacks on northern Israel, provoking massive military retaliation and an 18-year Israeli occupation of the south of the country. In doing this, Israel used the Palestinian raids also as a pretext to realise its old designs for 'regime change' towards a more Israel-friendly Lebanese government dominated by Maronite Christians. The 1982 Israeli bombing and six-month siege of Beirut led to the loss of some 20,000 Lebanese and Palestinian lives. The Israeli Army destroyed ministries, institutions and homes, as if aiming to wipe out the Lebanese state itself. For years, the Israeli self-styled 'security zone' in the south of Lebanon cut it off from the rest of the country, and turned it into a battlefield with ruined farmlands and a flood of refugees going northwards to Beirut. The cost of all this to Lebanon was unquantifiable, but must have run into billions of dollars, none of which was ever recovered in compensation from the Jewish state (or anyone else).

Jordan was home to the largest number of Palestinian refugees, estimated in 2021 at 5 million registered with the United Nations Relief and Works Agency (UNRWA). A further 300,000 Palestinians, displaced as a result of the 1967 war, also took refuge in Jordan. The cost of maintaining the camps, where many refugees had lived since their original displacement in 1948, was borne by the host country and the international community through UNRWA (for refugees registered with it, which did not represent the total number). For example, it was estimated that in 1998 the Jordanian government was spending an annual $250 per refugee on education, health and employment to UNRWA's $56, and in 2001, Jordan's expenditure was five times of UNRWA's.[23] In 2021, Jordan's expenditure on refugees was $1 billion annually, again more than UNRWA's.[24] Such costs, especially given the chronic deficit in UNRWA's budget, (made more acute by US President Trump's cut to all funding in 2018), were a considerable burden to the small economies of states like Jordan and Lebanon.

Nor did they take account of the additional social, political and security costs incurred by the presence of a displaced, politicised population with a commitment to fight for its rights. The Palestinian presence in the countries that were host to it was not one of immigrants seeking a better life. It was an uncomfortable, potentially destabilising intrusion into the body politic of these states, which had to accommodate it in different ways, all of which entailed some degree of disturbance to them. At no time did Israel offer compensation to these countries, but on the contrary demanded restitution for its Jewish citizens allegedly made refugees by various Arab states.[25] From an Arab (as apart from a Palestinian) point of view, a resolution of the situation without further Arab cost was long overdue.

Even had Arab governments, tied as they were to Western powers, wished to ignore Israel's treatment of the Palestinians, their own public opinion was always a factor to be taken into account. The mass of Arab people, even those as far away as Morocco,[26] was deeply sympathetic to the Palestinian cause, although to a lesser extent in recent years. The official Arab position on the Palestinians has remained one of declared support and solidarity precisely because of this factor. The 2003 war on Iraq, widely unpopular among Arabs, and the blatant partisanship that the Bush administration displayed towards Israel, only reinforced popular feeling. (One possible exception was Kuwait, whose people were outraged by Iraq's 1991 invasion and grateful for the US liberation of their land, although they also went on to expel almost all of Kuwait's resident Palestinian population of 400,000.) Arab governments, moreover, were not unaware of the danger to themselves from the rise of extremist Islamic movements that espoused the Palestinian cause. The growing instability inside Arab societies that reflected dissatisfaction with their governments' lack of public accountability, reliance on the enemies of the Arab people (the West and through it, Israel) and, by extension, colluded with the oppression of the Palestinians, was a potential danger. It followed that a resolution of the Palestinian problem would crucially remove one of the prime ingredients of this dangerous cocktail.

So the Arab regimes' conundrum was how to effect this, given the restrictions on their freedom of manoeuvre by, on the one hand, their dependence on Western aid, technology and trade, and especially on American favour, itself tied to their compliance over accommodating Israel – not as a normal state in the region, but as a superpower with a military and economic edge over them.[27] On the other hand, there was Israel's uncompromising and threatening stance and its rejection of all efforts at Arab accommodation, except on its own unacceptable terms. This was an unenviable dilemma which the Arabs' floundering, disunited policies and uncoordinated reactions did little to resolve.

Their irresolute and wavering stand had the result that Israel was allowed to impose its unique version of 'peace' on the Arab world, with all the Arab states pacified or disabled, including the potential challengers, Iraq and Syria, and the Palestinians almost bludgeoned into submission. It must have looked to the Western powers, which were instrumental in helping Israel to attain this achievement, as if they had finally succeeded in forcing Israel down the Arabs' throats, no matter what the Arabs themselves might have hoped or wished for.

CHAPTER THREE

Israel and the Jews

The relationship between Israel and a majority of world Jewry was historically close and essential to Israel's survival. The depth of that connection is likely to form a formidable obstacle to any suggestion of Israel's disestablishment through the creation of a shared Palestinian-Israeli state in its place.

It is difficult to find a phenomenon, historical or modern, comparable to the case of Israel. Here was a state, more in concept than actuality, with a unique appeal to religious, historical and psychological sentiment and an army of devoted followers, unprecedented in scale, working diligently on its behalf. The extent to which ordinary Jews, usually without the least intention of emigrating to Israel, nonetheless identified with it as an ideal, was astonishing. This identification first became overt, or for some Jews may have even started, in the wake of the Six-Day War. It was commonplace to see members of the Jewish community in the US and in many European countries volunteering to provide all sorts of services for the embattled Israelis (as they saw them).

The American Jewish community in particular had shown itself to be ardently Zionist and was a major direct donor to Israel, as well as its active proponent in US society and politics. Many American Jews who came to the US from Eastern Europe early in the twentieth century brought with them a distinctive religious/ethnic culture, which defined them in religious and national terms. Zionism, by combining secularism with religious tradition, must have been an immensely attractive ideology. Israel became the focus of identity for many

American Jewish groups, gave them a sense of communal cohesion and created networks amongst them. It also made them feel almost like other immigrants in America who had a home country to which they could visit or 'return'. Such psychological attachment is hard to forgo. It intensified after the 1967 and 1973 wars, reinforcing the perception that the Jews were about to be annihilated again for a people still profoundly affected by the Holocaust.[1] Between 1973 and 2002, it is estimated that US Jewish organisations bought a combination of Israel bonds and grants worth over $50 billion.[2] In 2016, Israel bond sales in the US reached an annual high of $1.27 billion.[3] Washington's foremost pro-Israel lobby, the American Israel Public Affairs Committee (AIPAC) campaigned energetically on Israel's behalf in the US Congress and collaborated with the Confederation of Presidents of Jewish Organisations, a powerful US group which coordinated the efforts of Jewish organisations on Israel's behalf.[4]

For these Jews, even at their most liberal, Israel had taken on a mythic quality, part-identity, part-religion, and its dissolution, *as a Jewish state*, became psychologically and emotionally unthinkable. The head of the Movement for Jewish Reform in Britain expressed this feeling well in 2005. 'When attacked,' he wrote, 'we [Zionists] respond by equating anti-Zionists with anti-Semites ... [It] wells up out of anger and frustration at not being allowed to be ourselves.' If Israel no longer existed, he said, it would be the end of Judaism too.[5]

Though many Zionist supporters were later prepared, and especially with the ascendance of right-wing governments in Israel after 2001, to criticise Israeli policies and display considerable sympathy for Palestinian suffering, all this was still predicated on the crucial assumption of the rightness and necessity of Israel's existence. Such people would not have felt constrained to find fault with Israel under a more benign regime, as say that of Yitzhak Rabin. His peacemaking actions in signing the Oslo Agreement in 1993, won their approval and, in equal measure, their dismay at his assassination in 1995.

Jews inside Israel, with the possible exception of a small minority of anti-Zionists – contemptuously labelled 'self-hating Jews' – naturally feared the end of Zionism. For them, the dissolution of a state predicated on an aspiration to exclusive Jewish membership (notwithstanding the 20 per cent Arab minority and the non-Jewish Soviet immigrants), and preferential treatment of Jews was not an option. These privileges were hugely augmented by US funding, (more than £3.8 billion annually in 2022) and world Jewish support.[6] Not least amongst these were the non-ideological settlers in the 'commuter settlements' of the West Bank, where inducements of cheap housing, tax breaks and jobs in Israel drew large numbers of young people who could not otherwise have attained the same standard of living in Israel or outside.[7] In many of the settlements I have seen, the houses were well laid out with neat roads and trees and, as they were built on hills, the views were often very beautiful. Where could such people dream of being so comfortably and picturesquely housed? Likewise, the settlements built on Syria's Golan Heights had yielded prosperity for those Jews who had farmed them since 1967.[8] Even though the economic situation suffered some reversals due to the 2000 Intifada, with poverty levels in Israel higher than at any time before, the average Israeli household still enjoyed a considerable edge over its Arab neighbours.[9] In 2018, before the Covid epidemic in Israel, 45.3 per cent of Arab families were described as living below the poverty line, as opposed to a much lower 13.4 per cent of Jewish families.[10] Given this disparity, Israelis would have vigorously rejected any threat of change to their special situation.

Within this general context, specific sectors of the Israeli Jewish population had their own additional reasons for

wanting to preserve the status quo. Religious Jews, and especially those amongst them who formed the bulk of religious
settlers in the West Bank colonies, believed passionately in the
concept of 'Eretz Israel', that every Jew had a God-given right
to the whole land between the Jordan River and the Mediterranean Sea. For this group, the Jewish state was a theological
imperative and, as evidenced by their strident opposition to
the government evacuation of Jewish settlements, however
small, in the Sinai in 1979 and those in Gaza in 2005, they
could barely conceive of giving up any part of the land they
considered Jewish.

These settlers formed some of the most vociferous, intractable and hardline supporters of the Jewish state. Mostly fanatical
ultra-orthodox Israelis or Jewish immigrants from the US,
they were widely feared by Palestinians for their unprovoked
aggression against them and vicious anti-social behaviour.
Baruch (formerly Barry) Goldstein, the ultra-religious fanatical Hebron settler of American extraction, who murdered 24
Arab Hebronites at prayer in the Ibrahimi Mosque in February
1994, received adulation by such people. After his killing by
angry Arab worshippers as a consequence, other settlers of
Goldstein's ilk (and many secular Jews in addition) went on
to idolise him and revere his tomb, which became a shrine for
them.[11] The settlers' notoriously sadistic harassment of Palestinians in Hebron provided further evidence of this behaviour.

But quite apart from all this, Israel had acquired a population of Israelis, and especially the younger generation
born there, so-called 'Sabras', who regarded Israel as their
natural home, and indeed, now had nowhere else to go. Not
long before, the number of those born in the state was lower
than those born outside, but by the 1990s that was no longer
the case.[12] Although in the years since the beginning of the
Second Intifada, a considerable number of Israelis emigrated
abroad, said to be higher than at any time since the founding

explained, if their origins were indeed Mediterranean. By the nineteenth century, more than half the world's Jews were to be found in Lithuania/Poland.[15] How did they get there in such large numbers? It is improbable that a Middle Eastern people would have gone out of choice to settle in the harsh, cold climate and environment of Eastern Europe so different from their own, although we do know that Jews, fleeing persecution under the Byzantine Empire, had gone to the Caucasus in early medieval times. But their numbers were small, and some other explanation must be found.

The Khazar hypothesis – that European Jews were descended from large-scale conversions to Judaism in Khazaria in early medieval times – was in vogue in the last century. Its chief proponent was Arthur Koestler, and a group of other writers.[16] However, these ideas were subsequently contested and largely discarded, and no plausible explanation for the phenomenon of European Jewry has emerged.[17]

What is not plausible, however, is that an unbroken chain existed between the Jews of Palestine and those of Europe, albeit with several stations in between, as if they had been sealed packages posted from one place to the other, their contents unchanged over the centuries. Put like this, the absurdity of the idea is obvious, but that in fact was the proposition Zionists wanted people to believe in order to justify the Jewish 'return' to the 'homeland'. Accepting anything else would have invalidated a central plank of the Zionist claim to Palestine, which had been instrumental in marshalling Western Christianity to its support.

Are Jews a separate racial/ethnic group? There is a confusion over this question which has persisted because many Jewish communities, by reason of the social strictures historically placed on them in various societies, often lived together and intermarried, perpetuating certain religious and other customs. Yet, with the possible exception of the East European

Ashkenazim whose claim to ethnicity was the strongest, Jews might at best have been described as societal sub-groups, or sects, like the Punjabi Sikhs, who have developed a strong ethno/national identity but yet are not a nation, or the Amish, an American Christian sect that keeps its adherent separate from mainstream society. One can see how such groups can come to occupy a special category, neither a separate nation nor quite natives.

Nevertheless, it is undeniable that many Jews saw themselves as part of a nation, race, or at least of one people in a way that Christians or Muslims did not. There are several components to the view that Jews were a separate people. In part, it had to do with the Orthodox Jewish position that Jews were only those born of a Jewish mother, which when adhered to, gave Jews a peculiar genetic/religious character. Such people were considered Jews even if they converted or renounced the faith, in which case they became 'apostates'. According to the Talmud, 'A Jew who has sinned still remains a Jew.'[18] Partly this was due to the Classical Reform view, largely faded today, that Jews were those who practiced Judaism; in other words, performed the *mitzvot*, a large number of daily religious duties the faithful must fulfil. And partly there was the view that antisemitism was the glue that defined Jews and made them stick together as one people.

Arabs, however, always saw the Jews as a religious group, especially in Palestine where they were regarded as ethnically part of the community; they spoke Arabic and had an Arab culture. As the Palin Commission set up by Britain to investigate the 1920 Arab–Jewish riots in Jerusalem remarked, 'The Orthodox Jew of Palestine were ... hardly distinguishable from the rest of the peasant population.'[19] Anyone familiar with Israelis from Arab countries will observe how culturally 'Arab' they are, or at least the older generations. The European Jews, however, who began to infiltrate Palestine from 1880 onwards, struck Arabs (and also the indigenous Jewish minority in Palestine) as foreigners and quite unlike what they termed as 'our Jews'. They looked different, behaved differently and spoke other languages

For Arabs, it was apparent that Eastern and Western Jews were so dissimilar as to throw doubt on the whole notion of their being one people. And yet, from my own observation growing up amongst European Jews in London, it was clear they genuinely believed themselves to be just that. And they were right in the sense that many of them could say they belonged to a loose affiliation of Ashkenazi East European Jews with similar histories, culture and a Yiddish language that the older generation all spoke. The people who gave birth to political Zionism, first established it in Palestine and dominated the Jewish state from its inception, were all members of this group.[20] They mostly came from the countries of Eastern Europe where most of them, especially those from Lithuania/ Poland, Russia and Ukraine, had developed a strong sense of ethnic identity. This was based on 'Yiddishism', a socio-political movement to develop Yiddish culture in Eastern Europe where the Ashkenazim lived. Over time, this community produced an impressive Yiddish literature and a thriving popular culture, as well as an important research institute at Vilna (Vilnius). There was, moreover, some genetic basis to their ethnic claim in the frequent association of certain inherited disorders, for example, Tay-Sachs disease, with Ashkenazi Jews. Even so, and although there was enough of a shared cultural and historical experience between them as to persuade many of them that they were a national group, it would be wrong to see them as such.

It was this Ashkenazi culture that was described to me as 'Jewish', when growing up in Britain in the 1950s. One could recognise it in its 'Jewish jokes', a black humour which recalled life in the *shtetl* (Yiddish for towns and hamlets in

Eastern Europe to which Jews were confined), its strange linguistic constructions of English mixed with Yiddish, its cuisine (chopped liver, gefilte fish, bagels) and its tradition of orthodox Jewish attire for men; the sight of black-coated Orthodox Jews in silk breeches and round fur hats, as if they had just stepped out of eighteenth-century Poland, walking to synagogue on Saturdays was typical and familiar to me living in Golders Green, at the time London's most Jewish suburb. Little did I understand when I met the Jewish girls at my school, with their German surnames and Yiddish vocabulary, that their forebears or relatives bore a responsibility for my expulsion from Palestine. Unwittingly putting my finger on the essence of the problem, I saw not the faintest connection between them and my homeland and therefore no reason for any hostility between us.

Ashkenazim became familiar in the West after the great waves of Jewish immigration from Russia and Eastern Europe at the turn of the twentieth century; had it remained at that, they might have gone down in history as a remarkable and interesting community with a rich culture to add to the wealth of human experience, but nothing more. As it was, political Zionism intervened with a definition of Jewish nationhood that was in reality nothing other than the ethnic Ashkenazi identity grafted onto the rest. In other words, the East European Ashkenazim reinterpreted themselves as the pan-Jewish nation, an imagined community with a fabricated unifying narrative. (Israel's national anthem, it may be noted, was nothing other than a medley of nostalgic Russian tunes.) It was for that reason that generations of non-Ashkenazi Jews who were brought to populate the new Jewish state after 1948 were subjected to what one might call 'Ashkenazification', an acculturation process to make them more like 'real' or European Jews. But the most egregious aspect of this false Ashkenazi representation of 'the Jewish people' was the claim it then made for a primordial connection with Palestine. That this became, as we shall see below, the received wisdom amongst Jews (and others) after Zionism had taken hold, makes it no less absurd and, for Palestinians, no less pernicious.

The idea of Jewish nationhood had great persuasive power in promoting the takeover of Palestine. But even had it been true that the origin of Jews in the world today, wherever they lived and no matter what they looked or sounded like, had been in Palestine 2,000 years ago, it is inconceivable that such a fact could ever have conferred on them the right of claiming it for themselves after all that time and to the detriment of its indigenous inhabitants. The history of humankind is littered with the movement of peoples and tribes from place to place, with changing patterns of habitation and repeated migrations. No one, other than the Zionists and their supporters, suggests that reversing this history would be either workable or desirable.

Yet the idea of a single Jewish people whose physical origin lay in the Middle East took tenacious hold of Jews themselves, irrespective of their personal histories, mother tongues, or secular cultures. Part of the reason lies in the very definition of Jewishness. To be a member of the Jewish faith is not just to subscribe to a set of religious beliefs; it also means laying claim to a specific history: the history of the Israelites according to the Old Testament, from their Abrahamic origins in the region we call the Middle East today, through to their 'dispersal' from it. This is reflected in the major Jewish religious festival of Passover which commemorates supposed historical events, in this case the Israelites' exodus from Egypt; the festival of Tisha b'Av marks the destruction of the Jewish temples in Jerusalem, and several other less important Jewish festivals also relate to biblical/historical accounts. To be a Jew is to be physically descended, however distantly, from this chain of *historical* events – that is, to be the bearer of a specific history, even if it is not accompanied by religious belief. When

Khazar converts to Judaism visited the Prince of Kiev in 986, they told him that their native land was Jerusalem and that they were a part of the dispersion of the Judeans.[21]

Grasping this fact is essential to understanding the nature of the situation, which is quite unlike that of the other major religions. To be a Christian or a Muslim is to subscribe to a set of precepts as laid out in these religions; it is not to say that Christians or Muslims are physical descendants of the Virgin Mary or the Prophet Muhammad or had any historical link with Palestine or the Arabian Peninsula respectively. Thus, conversion to these religions merely entails accepting relevant beliefs, but in the Jewish case orthodox and conservative doctrine has it that the convert must undertake to adopt the Jewish religious way of life and be accepted *as a member of the Jewish people*. He or she makes a commitment to integrate into the Jewish community by changing their religious *and ethnic* identity. This is problematic, since historical linkage cannot really be transferred. Yet to inherit this particular history was an essential component of being a Jew. This is encapsulated in Jewish religious teaching mentioned above, which stipulates that a Jew remains so even if he converts to another faith or becomes an atheist.

Such ideas no doubt helped promote the concept of a biologically linked, single people. But it was not just Jews themselves who nurtured these beliefs. They were immeasurably assisted, some would say created, by Christian attitudes towards them, especially in Europe. For example, the 1922 White Paper, the so-called 'Churchill Paper', that defined Britain's responsibilities to a Jewish national home in Palestine as propounded by the Balfour Declaration five years before, sought the establishment of 'a centre in which the Jewish people as a whole may take, on grounds of religion *and race* an interest and a pride' [emphasis added]. For centuries, Jewish communities in Europe were regarded as foreign bodies in the societies in

44

which they lived, were confined to specific localities and were frequently described in racial terms. This made their position anomalous and ambiguous, neither in nor out of the wider society. In this context, they also developed their own dialects, and hence the appearance of Judeo-Spanish (Ladino), and Judeo-German (Yiddish).

It was not until the European Enlightenment, that ushered in liberal and egalitarian social ideas, that Jewish communities in the eighteenth and nineteenth centuries started to break free of the confines of the ghetto and to integrate with the larger society. Jewish emancipation in Europe thus followed the spread of these liberal ideas and was most pronounced in Western Europe, where after the French Revolution Jews were granted equality before the law.[22] With the separation of church and state, official Jewish activity was confined to the religious sphere and the stereotyping of Jews as foreign elements began to break down. Increasing assimilationist tendencies amongst Jews, most marked in Germany, France and Britain, led to a greater identification between them and the national groups they lived amongst. For example, German replaced Yiddish in Germany and by the eighteenth century, Jewish children were beginning to receive a secular education.[23]

The assimilation process faced much greater barriers in Eastern Europe, where the hold of traditional Judaism was strong and the Jewish communities there had a quasi-ethnic identity of their own. The majority of Eastern European Jews lived in ghettos, apart from their non-Jewish compatriots, and traditionally led separate lives. As the Russian socialist revolutionary movements developed during the nineteenth century, Jews became particularly active participants and were gradually secularised. Towards the end of the century, they had broken through into Russia's economy and culture, although not as deeply as Jews had done in Western Europe.

At the same time, Jewish assimilationism in Europe provoked the creation or worsening of powerful anti-Jewish movements in Russia and elsewhere, to which the term 'anti-Semitism' (more often nowadays 'antisemitism') was first applied in modern times. There was a complexity of reasons for this discrimination against the Jews, made official policy in nineteenth-century Russia and in the Austrian Empire, where they had the status of citizens of the second or third category.[24] But the overall trend amongst Jews was emancipationist and a move away from the segregation and ghettoisation of the past. How this trend might have developed into our own time we cannot know, since it was dramatically interrupted by the appearance of Nazism in Central Europe, culminating in the Holocaust, that was to be a seminal event in halting, or even reversing, the process. Zionism itself was a response to the episodes of antisemitism that continued to plague Jewish communities in Europe, and though it attracted only a minority of Jews until the 1940s, it was a phenomenon striving towards the same de-assimilationist end. Since its establishment, Israel has acted as a counterweight to Jewish assimilation, which is the greatest threat to Zionism.

As is well known, most Jews were not initially interested in Zionism, seen as a fringe movement, nor were they interested in emigrating to Palestine. Its earliest opponents were no less than the Bund, a prominent Jewish socialist party founded towards the end of the nineteenth- century. Drawn from Russia, Lithuania and Poland, the Bund believed in creating centres of Jewish national-cultural autonomy within those countries, in contrast to Zionism, which the Bund opposed; the 'Jewish homeland', if there were to be any, should be set up, not in Palestine, but in the Pale of Settlement (stretching from Lithuania to Poland and Ukraine).[25] Only a tiny percentage of the millions of East European Jews who fled the Russian pogroms before the First World War went to Palestine. The majority of those that remained preferred universalist solutions to the narrow ideals of Zionism.[26] The German Orthodox and Reform Jewish communities also opposed it, as did the majority of European Jews, who saw no reason to leave their comfortable homes for a malaria-ridden backwater like Palestine. Nazism in Germany and the Holocaust had an enormous impact in reversing this reluctance, and Jewish immigration into Palestine and support for Zionism increased dramatically during the 1930s and in the wake of the Second World War. Jews began increasingly to identify with Israel's cause from the state's establishment in 1948, thanks to an active campaign funded by US Jews to promote this result. But it was not until 1967 that the process become so marked. The Six-Day War, and perhaps more significantly, the war of 1973 in which the Arabs fought more effectively, engendered in Jews an acute concern for Israel's survival. As the American Jewish writer Michael Novick noted, 'The hallmark of the good [American] Jew became the depth of his or her commitment to Israel.'[27]

The Jewish state came to assume a special status for the majority of Jews as the place of origin, the reference point and the untouchable ideal whose maintenance and survival were a sacred duty. Elie Wiesel, the ardent defender of Jewish Holocaust victims, who lived in the US, summed up this extraordinary commitment, 'I feel as a Jew who resides outside Israel I must identify with whatever Israel does – even with her errors. That is the least Jews in the Diaspora can do for Israel: either speak up in praise, or keep silent.'[28] Did this come about because of a Zionist propaganda effort, or for some other reason? There is no doubt that a massive campaign of publicity, persuasion and arm-twisting was fought ceaselessly on Israel's behalf. Much of the Jewish community and the wider society, especially in the US (whose collective guilt over the Holocaust was expiated in this way), were drawn into this propaganda effort – delegations visited Israel, along with the establishment of youth groups, academic exchanges, networking with centres of influence and power, media presentations, pro-Israel events and the like. 'Birthright Israel', for example, was an organisation that aimed to lure young Jews to holiday in Israel free of charge. This was considered an effective way to bind the Jewish Diaspora to the 'homeland'. Without these unrelenting efforts, some have argued, support for Israel might have waned, and Jews living outside might not have developed such identification with Israel.

Such tactics doubtless form an important part of the story, but they also build on a psychology that was already there amongst Jews, both religious and secular. The Israeli Marxist writer Akiva Orr has argued that the aim of political Zionism, a secular movement that arose in Eastern Europe, was to solve the identity problem of non-religious Jews. (For the religious, he wrote, it was not an issue: their reference point was Judaism and its rituals.) It was the secular Jews who had this identity problem, the product of a history of exclusion and alienation in European society. They saw themselves as different, even when there was no persecution, but could not define their identity with reference to religion, especially after the emancipation which weakened the hold of Judaism as an identity. Hence their need to establish a nation state which would provide an alternative secular identity for Jews like them.[29] Zionism therefore strove to provide a non-religious definition of Jewishness, and hence the emphasis from the beginning on Israel being a state like any other, 'as Jewish as England is English' (to quote Israel's first president, Chaim Weitzman), with a national, secular identity. Orr concludes that this still does not solve the problem of 'who is a Jew?', nor of those Jews living outside the state of Israel, whose identity remains ambiguous.

Yet, there was a need amongst European Jews for recognition of their separateness, not by way of the ghetto, but as a distinct group with a long tradition and a history of intellectual achievement. And behind that was the background of an accepted narrative about the continuity of the 'Jewish people', their ancient origins in biblical Palestine and worldwide dispersal from it that greatly assisted the ideology Zionism had created to take hold. As Ben-Gurion said apropos of the newly drawn up Israeli Law of Return in 1951, 'This right originates in the unbroken historical connection between the people and the homeland.' Though this appealed more to religious Jews, the concepts were familiar and to a certain extent influential with the non-religious as well. As has been explained to me in interviews, such people, rejecting any theological affiliation with Judaism, nevertheless would identify themselves as 'cultural Jews', that they belonged to a community with a shared history and 'ethnicity' and one with an outstanding contribution to Western society. This conviction, which is chiefly found amongst Ashkenazi Jews, apparently defies questions of differences in geography, mother tongue, customs, physical appearance, or local conditions. A non-religious Jewish writer of Polish parentage living in London illustrated this when she asserted to me that whenever she came across a Jew anywhere in the world, 'whether black-skinned or slant-eyed', she felt an instant affinity. This feeling, which was clearly genuine amongst the communities in parts of Europe, did not explain where they thought Oriental Jews, so un-European, fitted into this 'culture'.

After 1967, a majority of Jews came to accept Zionist dogma at face value and also to see Israel as a safe haven from persecution, real or imagined, despite its being the most unsafe place on earth for them. Israel had already fought four wars or been in a state of war with all of its neighbours for most of its existence. Jews who had had no opinion on Zionism, or even opposed it previously, also held this view. A striking example of this was a well-known British biologist of Jewish extraction

I knew in London, who was brought up by a socialist father with no time for nationalism of any kind, including Zionism. He was astounded to find this same father changed into an avid supporter of Israel in his declining years. He travelled to Israel for the first time in the late 1980s. 'You must cherish Israel with all your heart. It's our home and our refuge,' he told his son.

Growing up in Britain after 1949, I could see the transformation from 1967 onwards in the Jewish community, which had until then merged into the fabric of British society with considerable success. It had been a difficult process, and anti-Jewish sentiment still survived in certain institutions and amongst individuals until the 1960s, but the general climate of opinion was favourable and became increasingly liberal towards Jews over the next three decades. However, many Jews started to identify with the cause of Israel as 'the motherland' and to make no secret of their affiliation to it to the point that they took on its moral values as well. Such Jews regularly defended Israeli human rights violations, and were able to find a justification for the country's savage assaults on its neighbours.

It is difficult to see how such a psychological suspension between two societies could be of ultimate benefit to non-Israeli Jewish communities. Nor could this phenomenon be divorced from a rising rate of attacks on Jews and Jewish institutions in countries in both the East and West. Some of these at least were anti-Israeli in motivation, consequent on Israel's record of human rights abuse against the Palestinians, since Jews outside Israel were commonly and wrongly identified as universal supporters of the Jewish state as well as potential Israeli citizens. The 'ingathering of the exiles' was, after all, the central theme of Zionism. It should be no surprise that some non-Jews drew the obvious inference and targeted those they saw as surrogates for Israel.

The Zionist imperative to categorise all Jews as members of a separate and distinct race or nation, irrespective of where they lived, inevitably led to a blurring of the distinction between Israeli and non-Israeli Jews – and hence to view them as responsible for or complicit in Israel's policies. The tendency amongst many non-Israeli Jews to assume different identities as it suited them – now potential citizens of Israel, now English (or Italian or French or whatever) – only made this worse. Such dual identity is not unusual in today's pluralist Western societies; but in the Jewish case where 'Jew' and 'Israeli' or 'Zionist' are the categories of the second identity, it should not have been surprising that 'Jews', as a collective, should increasingly have become targets of hostile attacks against Israeli policy. This phenomenon led rapidly to accusations that anti-Zionism was being used as a surrogate for antisemitism.[30] But the reality was that so long as the drive towards closer ties with the Israeli state continued, Jews would continue to be surrogates for that state and hostile attitudes towards them for that reason would harden and increase.

The rise of anti-Jewish attacks in several European countries was seen as the resurgence of an old gentile affliction. In fact, such attacks in Europe increased sharply with the Second Intifada, suggesting a linkage with Israeli policy. After 2016, and the election in Britain of the Labour Party leader, Jeremy Corbyn, seen by Zionists as dangerously pro-Palestinian, and thus anti-Israel, the tendency to identify anti-Zionism as antisemitism became more established in Britain. The introduction of the International Holocaust Remembrance Alliance (IHRA) definition of antisemitism in the same year made the linkage between hatred of Jews and criticism of Israel explicit.[31] This definition, vague and not legally binding in structure, had appended to it eleven so-called 'illustrative examples' of antisemitism. These were mostly concerned with

CHAPTER FOUR

The Israeli-Palestinian 'Peace Process'

By 2021, finding a solution for a conflict that had blighted the lives and future, not just of Palestinians, but of the Arab world (and of Israel too) was more urgent than ever. The Palestinians, whose situation worsened by the day, could not afford more time while yet more futile attempts were made to find a solution. In the flare-ups that occurred in May 2021, Palestinian communities under Israeli rule in Jerusalem, Gaza, the West Bank and 1948 Israel rose up in protest together. Two hundred and fifty Palestinians were killed, and over a thousand were wounded, with massive destruction to Gaza's buildings and infrastructure. These depredations, added to the unacceptable prolongation of refugee life for millions of Palestinians, and Israel's dangerous efforts to destroy the Palestinian national cause were imperatives that demanded urgent action.

At the same time, Israel's power and dominance in the region and in the affairs of the world's only superpower had grown, as did the threat it posed to regional stability and beyond. Not surprisingly, the exceptional indulgence lavished on the Jewish state by the West had nurtured in Israelis powerful feelings of invincibility, self-importance and inflated ideas about Israel's place in the world. They had come to believe that the norms of international behaviour did not apply to Israel, which must be immune from censure and sanction, no matter what it did. A state armed with such beliefs and a powerful arsenal of conventional and nuclear weapons as well, is a very dangerous thing and a neighbour much to be feared.

Furthermore, Israelis, especially after the victory of 1967, were reared with a conviction that the whole of historical Palestine belonged to them, that the Palestinians had no right to the land but were there on sufferance, and that Israel's needs, whether for land, resources, or security, were paramount. For that reason every offering, however small, that Israel contemplated giving to the Palestinians was seen as a concession and a 'painful sacrifice' for peace. To use the popular jargon, there were two national narratives at work here, Israeli and Palestinian, in direct contradiction with each other. The power imbalance between the two parties ensured that the Israeli one always prevailed.

The overall situation has traditionally given little rise for optimism. The principal protagonists were hopelessly unequal, with the balance of forces heavily weighted in Israel's favour. The Palestinians on the other hand were not only weak and vulnerable in themselves, but their only backing derived, as we saw, from an Arab world ruled by governments which were themselves prey to Western influence and incapable of confronting Israel. It is difficult to avoid the conclusion that, given the line-up of conflicting forces, the outcome was foreordained. The conflict with Israel was becoming more intractable than at any time previously; numerous peace plans were put forward, while Israel's appropriation of land and resources went on relentlessly, squeezing the Palestinians into ever smaller areas, or pushing them to emigrate. The ensuing Palestinian resistance had met with brutal Israeli reprisals and widespread abuses of human rights. Unabashed American support for Israel in this volatile climate was almost incomprehensible in its folly and insouciance.

The Arab-Israeli peace process

There is no term in the political lexicon more bandied about and with less meaning than 'the Arab-Israeli peace process'. Earlier, the term referred mainly to a settlement between Israel and the Arab states, but since the Oslo Agreement of 1993, it increasingly came to denote specifically the process between Israel and the Palestinians, with the rest of the issues on hold. Yet, despite the passage of 74 years since the armistice of 1949 that ended the first Arab–Israeli war, no settlement, which would end all states of hostility and ensure a durable peace in the region, had been achieved. Numerous peace proposals came and went, but none succeeded in ending for good the multi-layered enmity between Israel and the Arabs.

Why was there no solution? Why did all the international and regional efforts, which often appeared so promising, fail to resolve the conflict? Up until 1993, when the Oslo Accords were signed between Israel and the PLO, peace negotiations were not principally about the Palestinian issue, although it usually featured somewhere. Of course, there was always an awareness, especially on the part of the Arabs, that this issue would have to be addressed, but it was not reflected in a primacy of commitment to it in any peace proposal. The prevailing attitude towards the Palestinian refugees is a good illustration of this: everyone knew in theory that they needed a just solution, but in practice, they were ignored, patronised, or looked down upon as lesser mortals. This principle has constantly animated the approach to the process of Arab-Israeli peacemaking.

Resolution 242

The famous but unimplemented UN Security Council Resolution 242, passed after the 1967 war, was the first serious international attempt at peacemaking between Israel and the Arabs. This resolution set the basis for all subsequent peacemaking efforts and reflected no mean achievement for Israel. While whittling down the Palestinian issue to one of refugees in an obliquely worded phrase – 'a just settlement of the refugee problem' – it offered Israel an end to the state of belligerency with the Arabs, a recognition of its sovereignty and territorial integrity and, by implication, opened the way to its eventual acceptance into the region.[1] Less than twenty years from its establishment, effected against tremendous Arab resistance and hostility, the state of Israel was being awarded an almost instant conversion from regional pariah to regional legitimacy and acceptance, with the Palestinians safely out of the way as a humanitarian problem awaiting a just solution, whatever that might mean. Unsurprisingly, the PLO rejected the resolution on those grounds and also because it made no mention of Palestinian sovereignty over Gaza and the West Bank after their being vacated by Israel.

Israel's obdurate manoeuvrings in the aftermath of this resolution would also be the pattern for the future. Not satisfied with what was already offered, it insisted on direct negotiations with the Arab states, one by one and without preconditions. The calculation was always the same, and it served Israel's strategy well: that the Arabs would not agree to such bilateral deals because they implied recognition of the Jewish state for no guaranteed reciprocal benefit, nor would they accept the exclusion from the talks of third parties to help secure any agreement reached. In the ensuing hiatus, Israel could continue to hold on to and settle Arab land, with resolution of the Palestinian issue deferred. The international community made few effective efforts to counter these Israeli ploys; no international mechanism was ever established to compel Israel to withdraw from Arab land, or to enforce its compliance with a realisation of Palestinian political and human rights.

Between 1967 and the Camp David Agreement

Earnest attempts were made to circumvent these handicaps but never came to anything. Much diplomatic activity followed the passing of Resolution 242, but by 1970, the US had come round to Israel's view: that only limited peace agreements with individual Arab states were possible. The Palestinian cause was put on the back burner, and the PLO retaliated by initiating its campaign of armed resistance against Israeli targets, first from Jordan and then, when its forces were driven out, from Southern Lebanon. The damaging effect of this move on the stability of Lebanon, its economy and its people over the following decades is well known.

Had international will prevailed in 1967 – that is, to face up to Israel and ensure its compliance over the issue of occupied Arab land and the crucial matter of Palestinian rights – perhaps the Middle East might have been spared much subsequent turmoil, bloodshed, destabilisation and war. As it was, any progress in resolving the conflict between Israel and the Arabs only came through a mixture of cajoling, bribery and coercion, always flawed by the insufficient attention paid to the Palestinian dimension. Every peace agreement was constructed at the expense of the Palestinians, although various parties tried to do something for them. US President Jimmy Carter displayed an initial willingness to resolve the Palestinian issue. In 1977, he proposed an international peace conference in conjunction with the USSR on the basis of Resolution 242, which was to include a solution for the Palestinian problem and recognition of 'the legitimate rights of the Palestinian people'. Israel would withdraw from most of the 1967 territories (though not all) and all states of belligerency would end, leading to a full peace and recognition between Israel and the Arab states. But Carter came under strong pressure from

57

the State Department, Israel and the US Zionist lobby and he was forced to abandon the international peace conference idea, since he was not prepared to exert any pressure on Israel to accept, as had become usual by now in the US's dealings with Israel.

Camp David and after

In the end, Egypt and Israel concluded a separate peace deal in 1979, in which the Palestinian dimension played a part in the peace talks. An autonomy plan for the occupied territories was discussed during exhaustive negotiations, which dragged on until 1980. The plan stipulated that, after a period of five years, in which the Palestinians in the West Bank and Gaza (though not East Jerusalem) would prepare for 'full autonomy', a self-governing Authority would be established through free elections. After this, and when the powers of the Authority were defined, Israel would then re-deploy its forces in the Palestinian territories. Three years from *this* point, final-status talks would begin on matters such as security, borders and other issues. No mention was made of Israel's withdrawal from the West Bank or Gaza; Jerusalem's status was left uncertain, and no reference was made to Israel's illegal settlements, nor to Palestinian national rights.

In 1981, Saudi Arabia put forward an 'Arab' peace proposal in the shape of the Fahd plan, but Israel ignored it. The Fahd plan proposed that, in line with Resolution 242, Israel withdraw from the 1967 territories and the Palestinians be granted a state on the West Bank and Gaza with East Jerusalem as its capital, and that all states in the region 'to live in peace'. In other words, the Arabs were offering an implied recognition of Israel in its pre-1967 borders and acknowledging West Jerusalem as a Jewish city (in contradiction to the

UN Partition Resolution of 1947 which assigned the city as neither Jewish nor Arab and to be administered by the UN).

Ronald Reagan followed the Fahd plan with his own proposal in 1982, which was much kinder to Israel. There was to be no Palestinian state or self-determination and no PLO participation, only an autonomy arrangement in confederation with Jordan. The Arabs responded by declaring the PLO the Palestinian people's 'sole legitimate representative'. Since the Arabs were in no position to enforce this or any other of their declarations, it made little impact. And still the Palestinian issue remained marginal to the process of peacemaking.

Finally, the Palestinians themselves declared their willingness to formally recognise Israel, although this had been implicit in their policy making from 1974 onwards. Following King Hussein of Jordan's surrender of the West Bank to the PLO in 1987, the Palestine National Council meeting held in Algiers a year later offered Israel mutual recognition and accepted what the PLO had previously always rejected, namely Resolutions 242 and 338. For the Palestinians, it was a major step and a world away from their previous ambition to liberate the whole of the land taken from them by the Zionists in 1948.

From there to Algiers in less than ten years was a huge step and a reflection of the reality on the ground that the PLO could not ignore: a powerful Israel with powerful backers, and a weak and disunited Arab front unable to fight Israel or support the Palestinians. Israel showed no interest in the PLO offer.

The Madrid peace conference

By 1991, Israel's strategy to strip the Palestinian cause of any meaning or significance, followed faithfully by the US against ineffective Arab opposition, seemed to be succeeding. Attempts to convene an international peace conference had come to nothing thus far, and Israel had been left to consolidate its hold on the Arab territories it occupied. But in the aftermath of the 1990–91 Gulf War, the US under the less partisan George Bush, Sr, was determined to resolve the Arab–Israeli conflict, as part of 'the new world order' he espoused. He was anxious that the Arab states, which had helped the Western coalition attack Iraq, expected no less. In October 1991, a major international peace conference was convened in Madrid.

The Madrid conference set up a series of multilateral talks, which sought to find solutions for major regional issues such as water rights, arms control, trade and refugees; these talks dragged on until 1993. As in the Camp David negotiations, the Palestinians were offered an interim agreement, which this time they accepted on condition that it would lead to an independent state. But, as before, Israel refused, agreeing only to an autonomy arrangement with land, security and foreign affairs under its own control. In the end, all these elaborate arrangements and diplomatic manoeuvrings came to nothing on both the Palestinian and Syrian fronts, (Israeli-Jordanian relations had experienced some positive progress), and the Madrid conference closed without a resolution of the conflict.

The Oslo Agreement

In 1993, the Palestinians themselves took over the function of peacemaking. This marks an important turning point in the history of the process. Although the PLO had been making proposals for coexistence with Israel since 1974 (all ignored), this time they were negotiating with the state of Israel directly and not through the customary intermediaries. Even so, as will be seen, the process they were able to effect with Israel was marked by the same failure to address the basis of the conflict, and they ended up as short-changed as previously. The byzantine bartering, dishonesty, evasion, cheating and relentless degradation of the Palestinian position that Israel indulged in throughout this process bears close study as an arch-demonstration of its demeaning and dismissive attitude. For Israelis, Palestinians were still 'non-people' and little had changed in that respect since the beginning of the Zionist project.

By 1993, the PLO had become irrelevant and virtually bankrupt. Successive traumas – its expulsion from Lebanon in 1982, the banishment of its leadership and fighters to Yemen and Tunis at the periphery of the Arab world, and the condemnation of its friendly stance towards Saddam Hussein in the Gulf War – meant that the PLO had little reputation and little money left. The Palestinians of the occupied territories, who had risen up against the Israeli occupation in 1987 independently of the PLO, were further unimpressed by that organisation's performance in the Madrid conference and the way it had meekly accepted its background role and the absurd offer of an interim agreement, which they could see gave Israel room to tighten its hold on their land. The fragmentation of the Palestinian front, which the Intifada had sharpened into those under occupation and those outside under an impotent and demoralised leadership, was proceeding apace. This was exactly in line with Israel's aspirations and many of its machinations over the years.

Thus, when secret talks began between the PLO and Israel in 1992 in the run-up to the Oslo Agreement, the standard interpretation has it that Yasser Arafat was looking for a role and wanted to make the PLO relevant again, while Yitzhak Rabin, Israel's Labour Party leader elected in 1972, was looking to offload Gaza, the rebellious, overcrowded and impoverished colony which was more trouble than it was worth. Arafat provoked the ire of many Palestinians, who felt he had sold out to the Israelis for personal gain.

The impact of the Intifada had made Rabin realise that the Palestinians were never going to disappear, or leave Israel undisturbed. The militant Islamist groups, Hamas and Islamic Jihad, had now become prominent as a force. In addition, Rabin thought that the Palestinians would eventually put the Zionist nature of the Jewish state at risk – by demographic increase, growing interchange between the two sides, perhaps even by the occupied Palestinians one day demanding equal civil and political rights with Israelis – a risk that was too great to ignore. He thus sought to preserve Zionism, in a smaller geographical space if necessary, as long as it left intact a 'Jewish Israel'. He did this by implementing the doctrine of separation (Hebrew, *hafradah*), that is, ensuring a clear, physical division between the two sides. Confined to their own space, the Palestinians were free to construct an entity of some sort, which could take on all the appurtenances of a state and call itself what it liked.

The Oslo Agreement, signed in Washington in 1993 with the pomp and ceremony that would have been more fitting to a final and comprehensive resolution of the Arab–Israeli conflict than the limited deal it was, were concluded between a state on the one hand and an organisation on the other. The Oslo Agreement meant that Arafat, supposedly representing the entire Palestinian nation, signed up to recognise Israel's right to exist in peace and security, to renounce and control 'terrorism', and to delete those parts of the PLO Charter deemed hostile to Israel. Essentially, the PLO recognised Israel as a state, but received no reciprocal Israeli recognition of the Palestinian right to statehood.

And thus Israel had been awarded the greatest prize it could ever have hoped for, something that had eluded it since its establishment. At one stroke, in signing the Agreement, Arafat had legitimised Zionism, the very ideology that had created and still perpetuates the Palestinian tragedy. Of course, Israel had managed quite well without the need for such recognition, but for the very people whose lives had been ruined by Israel's creation to extend their blessing to their own ruin was like the icing on the cake

The Oslo Agreement had started out as a bold Palestinian attempt to take matters into their own hands and directly confront Israel. And indeed the Agreement had at first generated great optimism amongst Palestinians, accompanied by an equally powerful hostility towards its detractors, who were condemned as 'enemies of peace'. But forging such an agreement turned out to be more difficult than they could have imagined. Israel repeatedly reneged on its deadlines and it became clear that the areas eventually handed over to Palestinian 'rule' enjoyed no Palestinian sovereignty at all. Even Arafat was required to have Israel's permission every time he flew his helicopter from one place to another, since the air space over the occupied territories belonged to Israel. All entry and exit to the territories was likewise controlled by Israel, despite a risible arrangement meant to placate the Palestinians, where Palestinian officials would carry out the security checks on travellers, while Israeli guards remained invisible behind dark screens, monitoring the officials and overruling their decisions at will.

Israel's agreements with the Palestinians left Israel in control of the borders, the air space and the settlements; the Israeli Army could move freely along all roads and had security jurisdiction over every aspect of Palestinian life. Not surprisingly, the tortuous process of negotiation, with its stops and starts and offers made and then withdrawn, was punctuated by Palestinian violence against Israeli targets, each time provoking the usual excessive Israeli mass reprisals. And each time, Israel would demand that Arafat 'control the violence' and 'fight terrorism', a refrain made familiar by its over-use from then until the present day. At the same time, there was no similar Israeli undertaking with regard to settler violence or indeed the violence of Israel's own troops. (Gaza, for example, was under curfew from June 1993 until January 1994.) This notwithstanding, the main cities of Jenin, Tulkarm, Qalqilia, Ramallah and Nablus were eventually transferred to Area A and granted autonomy status over civil affairs. But Hebron, whose partial evacuation had to wait until 1997, was forced to retain the provocative enclave of hard-line Jewish settlers in the city's centre, guarded by thousands of Israeli soldiers.

Arafat's agenda

Why did Arafat and his colleagues accept these conditions, or indeed agree to the Oslo arrangement in the first place? Various reasons were put forward: Israel had recognised the PLO and thereby acknowledged the existence of a Palestinian people who needed a solution; Resolution 242 had been agreed as the basis of the peace process, emphasising the formula of 'land-for-peace' which should apply to the Palestinian territories as well. In addition, issues that Israel had managed to make taboo subjects – Jerusalem, settlements and refugees – were firmly on the negotiations agenda. These implications of the Oslo Agreement were strictly true, but any optimism they might have generated was short-lived. Palestinians could see for themselves – in the expansion of settlements, checkpoints and bypass roads – that the reality was different.

It was not that Arafat ignored these facts or, in his apparent acquiescence with Israel's creeping colonisation, was in the process of betraying the Palestinian cause, as some accused him. His real agenda transcended these considerations. He truly believed in the foot-in-the-door approach – that if Israel could be prevailed upon to allow a Palestinian rehabilitation, in the shape of the modest steps towards independence they sought, and thereby accord them recognition as a nation with rights – then this would form the first stage in a continuous process that would lead inexorably on to statehood.

So wedded was he to this concept that he subordinated every objection he might reasonably have made to Israel's hegemonic demands to the greater aim of maintaining the momentum towards inevitable statehood, as he saw it. He displayed an unseemly eagerness to accept every crumb that fell from Israel's high table, and a reluctance to use any kind of leverage against Israel to attain a better deal.[2] Arafat's basic premise was that the state of Israel was too powerful to be directly challenged. The only way to achieve Palestinian aims was to hoodwink it into entering a process, which, despite itself, would ultimately end in a Palestinian state. It was for this reason that the Palestinian Authority assumed the trappings of statehood, appointing ministers and establishing institutions, flying the national flag and creating a Palestinian currency and passport. At first sight, this seemed ridiculous in a situation of colonial occupation; it is less so when understood as the Palestinian version of 'creating facts', projecting an image to the world of a state-in-waiting which, however unpropitious the conditions seemed, would be difficult to set aside.

The pursuit of this policy drew the Palestinian leadership into a downward spiral of ever greater retreats, giving up more and more of their previous conditions for the sake of some settlement with Israel, and developing an abject dependence on the good offices of its powerful patron, the United States. Like Anwar Sadat before him (as well as all other Arab leaders), Arafat believed that the US held all the cards and sought its appeasement at almost any price. But, as always happened before, Israel was acutely aware of this position, and took increasing advantage of Arafat's weakness and Palestinian vulnerability to push its demands further for more concessions. Consequently, and as the peace process ran into increasing delays and difficulties, a number of attempts were made to resuscitate it. None of these met with any success and they were all similarly flawed: they dealt with the two parties as if they were equal and argued the position, not from a previous reference point based on principle, but from the point it had reached at that particular moment. Israel, which was adept at moving the goalposts each time, was the obvious beneficiary, and the Palestinians found themselves each time having to accept the new terms. And as before, Israel had the power to suspend or amend any part of the process, as it deemed fit. The old pattern of attempting to impose a settlement at the Palestinians' expense was now evident once again.

The Camp David talks

The peace process having stalled once again, a meeting at Egypt's Sharm al-Sheikh was convened between Israel and the Palestinians in September 1999, which produced what became known as the Sharm al-Sheikh, or Wye II, Memorandum.[3] But little had progressed on the Palestinian front. Final-status talks had not begun and the settlement-building programme was proceeding as briskly as ever. The Camp David negotiations of July 2000, instigated at American behest to try and achieve a final settlement, took place against this stalemate. Israel judged the Palestinians to be at their weakest and likely to be coerced into an agreement at any price, while US President Bill Clinton was anxious to arrive at a successful Middle East settlement before his term of office expired.

The meeting between Arafat and Israeli Prime Minister Ehud Barak, which involved an exhausting 14 days of the most intensive negotiation, arm-twisting, intimidation and coercion ever aimed at the Palestinians, ended in total failure. It is important to remember that the land that was the subject of negotiation was already extensively colonised by Israeli settlements, bypass roads and 'security areas'. The Palestinian Authority had control, in whole or in part, of over only 42 per cent of Palestinian territory. Israel now proposed to annex 10–13 per cent of the West Bank, which contained 90 per cent of the settlements. These were constituted as three massive blocs in the north, centre and south of the West Bank, and were to be expanded and connected to each other and to Israel via bypass roads that took yet more Palestinian land. It was no accident that the Israeli-held areas were precisely those where the West Bank's main water sources are located, so as to keep them firmly under Israeli control. Parts of the Jordan Valley would be retained as Israeli military areas, amounting to 14 per cent of West Bank territory, for 12 to 20 years. The Palestinian areas would be connected by a series of tunnels and bridges, and Hebron would remain divided. The result would be a non-contiguous Palestinian territory, with enclaves separated by strips of Israeli-held land.

As before, Israel rejected any suggestion of responsibility for the Palestinian refugees, either historically or morally. If there was to be a right of return, then it might be to a future Palestinian entity, although even that would have been in doubt, since Israel controlled all borders and air space and would take measures in case of any 'infiltration'. Any refugee return to Israeli territory was to be at Israel's own discretion entirely, and Barak spoke of a programme of gradual family reunion for a maximum of 10,000 refugees. Compensating the rest was acceptable, provided it came from an international fund at no cost to Israel (and from which, he proposed, Jews expelled from Arab countries after 1948 should also benefit). Not even a verbal apology or acknowledgement for the refugee tragedy was forthcoming from Barak.

And, after all that, the Palestinians were asked to sign a document declaring the end of conflict and a permanent cancellation of all outstanding claims they had against Israel. The protagonists' position on all the permanent-status issues were diametrically opposed, and the only arbiter who could minimise the differences was a party already deeply committed to Israel's imperatives and welfare. As became clear, Israel was not prepared to withdraw to the 1967 borders, would not remove the settlements, would not relinquish East Jerusalem, and rejected the Palestinian right of return. To bridge such divergent positions fairly was clearly going to be a Herculean task. In the event, nothing like that was even attempted at the Camp David summit, which seemed designed to draw the Palestinians into a dialogue based on an unequal relationship with Israel, weighted even more by the addition of the US as arbiter, in effect pitting one against two.

The Camp David proposals were an insult to the Palestinian cause. They were offered in the same mean spirit that had characterised the Oslo Agreement seven years before. As ever, the parameters were those of pauper and prince: the Palestinians must be grateful for whatever they could get, not as of right, but as largesse from Israel. If they asked for more, they might find themselves, like Oliver Twist, castigated for greed. This was the basic reality underlying the statesman-like rhetoric at Camp David and the pretence it gave of a proper contractual process between equivalent parties. That this just and legal cause should have been so traduced by the insatiability and arrogance of an over-confident Israel, backed by a pliant US, is a shaming indictment of all those who allowed it to happen. A review of what was negotiated at Camp David shows how paltry were the offers made to the Palestinians. Only those who saw them as paupers without rights, grateful for anything as better than nothing could possibly have thought otherwise.

The failure of the Camp David talks was an outcome of the utmost gravity for both Palestinians and Israelis. It led to the outbreak of the Second Intifada, which this time was armed and more violent than the previous one. In the ensuing five years, several attempts were made to halt the violence and return the parties to the negotiating table. It did not seem to occur to Israel or its supporters that making peace on the basis of unequal power with a biased sponsor and minimal offerings was not a winning formula. Left to itself, Israel was content to continue appropriating land and resources and building settlements with a minimum of interference.

With the election of a new Israeli government under the hard-line Ariel Sharon, all negotiations ceased and the Intifada raged on. A US-initiated fact-finding committee under the chairmanship of former Senator George Mitchell in 2001 recommended, inter alia, that the Palestinian Authority (PA) should make an 'all-out effort' to control Palestinian violence and 'be seen by the government of Israel as doing so'; in return, Israel was to freeze settlement building and 'consider' withdrawing its forces to their positions as of 28 September 2000, the eve of the start of the Second Intifada. The parties were to return to the negotiating table 'in a spirit of compromise and reconciliation'.

The 'Road Map' was the name given to the next formula for Israeli-Palestinian peacemaking. Emanating from George Bush's call of 2002, it was elaborated into a phased plan which would lead to the creation of a Palestinian state. Its implementation was to be supervised and monitored by the Quartet – the US, Russia, the EU and the UN – within a short time frame, starting in 2003 and ending with a Palestinian state in 2005. The Road Map was a detailed and precise plan with defined stages, each of which was to be judged in terms of how the parties performed. Its three phases set out within specified time intervals a series of actions, which each side must undertake, and on the satisfactory performance of these, the next phase would begin.

Like the Oslo Agreement, it employed a futile gradualist approach, which concentrated on process more than substance. It came with no enforcement mechanism to ensure the compliance of the parties that was essential to its progress, and, despite the grand-sounding Quartet as supervisor and arbiter, the real decisions lay, as ever, with the US. More attempts to make the peace process yield results were initiated, but after 2014, when President Obama's envoy to the region, John Kerry, strained every sinew to bring the two sides together, peace negotiations came to an end.

* * *

In summary, no Israeli-Palestinian peace deal has worked to date, and efforts to revive peace talks have stalled. Nor is a change in this position likely, so long as the parameters of conventional peacemaking remain unchanged – namely, that it was possible to make a settlement which downgraded the Palestinian issue and delimited Palestinian rights, while it was not permissible to pressure Israel into conceding anything that went against its own wishes. If we put these two concepts together, bearing in mind the gross asymmetry of power between the two sides, the only settlement possible would be one imposed by the stronger party. The then-President Donald Trump's 2020 peace plan, misleadingly titled 'Peace to Prosperity: A vision to improve the lives of the Palestinian and Israeli people', was a case in point: this is what the 'peace process' between Israel and the Palestinians had been trying to do. Consequently, all the proposals put forward sought to satisfy Israel by sidestepping the Palestinian issue, ignoring its fundamental importance in the conflict, and proposing peace terms that were always at the expense of Palestinian rights. Even when, finally, the Palestinians themselves entered the process of peacemaking, their leadership was still prepared to sell them short in order to gain concessions from Israel. This process, which started with the gradual erosion of the aim to liberate the whole of Palestine into accepting just a part of it, culminated in Arafat's capitulation to the terms of the Oslo Accords for the reasons discussed above. Having taken this route, the decline to further Palestinian concessions and diminishing expectations was inevitable. This long history of marginalisation, part imposed but now also self-generated, has created, in both the minds of policymakers and in popular perception, the idea that a solution which falls far short of meeting the basic requirements of justice for the Palestinians would be sufficient.

The impetus to bargain away Palestinian fundamental rights in this way, though they were unassailably enshrined in law and common humanity, was the logical consequence of a Palestinian fear of total annihilation by Israel. It was a despairing strategy to salvage something from which to regenerate the remnants of Palestine, even though the price was high. Without this sacrifice, it seemed to Arafat and his successors that Israel would finish what it had started in 1948: the destruction of the Palestinian people, the loss of the land that remained to them and possibly their total expulsion. That matters should have come to this pass, of a people forced to de-legitimise their own national cause, renounce their legal rights and recognise the theft of their land by others as legally and morally acceptable (as implied in Palestine's recognition of Zionism), is the stuff of tragedy.

The Palestinians never posed any physical threat to Israel's continued existence. It was rather the fact of their moral power to invalidate Israel's claim to the same status – that of a legitimate nation in its own land – by their very existence as living witnesses to their own disinheritance. The near-hysterical Israeli reaction to any mention of a refugee return to Israel is motivated by this fear. So long as the Palestinian cause survived, a question mark would hang over the legitimacy of the Jewish state.

There is no doubt that Palestinian ineptitude and an inadequate leadership contributed to this depredation in Palestinian fortunes. For Arafat to have concluded that there was no alternative other than to surrender to Israel's demands (though not all), was a mistake. Palestinians had no formal power, it was true, but they had a negative power: to say 'no' to Israel's conditions at the Oslo Agreement and subsequently. The failure to exploit the fact that Israel would never have negotiated in 1993 had it not needed to – and it was that which gave the Palestinian veto its power – was a cardinal error. There is a whole story to be told about the mistakes, *naïveté* and sheer folly of Palestinian conduct, not to speak of the ineptitude, selfishness and timidity of the Arab governments – all of which played their deadly part in this tragedy. Even then, could the Palestinians' failure to defend themselves adequately against Israel have justified what was done to them? Where is it written that failure is a crime, deserving of punishment? While not stupid, nevertheless, the Palestinians had been required in the short space of a few decades to transform themselves from peasants and refugees into a modern people able to hold their own against the sophisticated challenges of dealing with Israel and its supporters. That they faltered and failed in various ways should not have been surprising. On the contrary, the only surprise was that they had come as far as they had.

The most important cause of Palestinian degradation and near destruction, however, was the ceaseless support and indulgence showered on the Jewish state by the US and Europe since its inception and before. A reassessment of this misguided policy and of where the Zionist project could lead was possible at several junctures in the history of the conflict over the last 75 years. But no one bothered, since the action needed to rectify the problem involved some hard questions about the nature of what had been created in the Middle East and a reversal of Western policy towards the Jewish state.

Thanks to this negligence, Israel succeeded in changing the occupied territories beyond recognition. It colonised and can-tonised them, erecting an impenetrable barrier wall to enclose and isolate these cantons, creating a series of ghettos inside which Palestinians festered, incapable of leading a normal life. Each community was separated from the others and hardly anyone could visit Jerusalem any more. Moving about 'ille-gally' through tortuous unpaved roads and tracks, which was the only alternative to perpetual imprisonment, took hours and carried considerable risks of discovery by Israeli patrols and at Israeli checkpoints.

Nothing that has been written here is new, mysterious, or hidden. The information is all in the public domain, available to anyone who cares to look, and is often exposed to public view through the media. How much better known it must have been to the myriad experts and specialists of the American and European governments! Israel never concealed (or halted) its colonisation programme of the Palestinian territories. It relentlessly judaised Jerusalem before the public eye, brazenly appropriating it as its capital and vociferously wearing down opposition to this illegal move. In broad daylight, Israel suc-ceeded in parcelling up the Palestinian territories into separate enclaves without physical means of connection. For decades, it openly changed facts on the ground, as if there had been no international law and no peace process. The results could be clearly seen on the numerous published maps of the occupied territories, showing a grid of Israeli settlements and bypass roads, as well as the barrier wall, all of which broke up the territory into a jigsaw of Israeli and Palestinian pieces. At the same time, Israeli human rights abuses against the Palestin-ians were shown on television, reported on by journalists, documented by human rights organisations, and observed by foreign diplomats, church and international groups, and a host of visitors.

If a Martian had dropped down onto the West Bank in this situation, he would have understood Israel's strategy at a glance and drawn the obvious conclusion from it: that there was no possibility of the chequered landscape he saw becoming one contiguous state for anyone. Yet, the official Western discourse was that it *was* possible and *would* happen. Western powers persisted in speaking of a 'road map' towards the creation of an 'independent, viable and contiguous' Palestinian state and went through the motions of trying to help create such a state.

It is not credible that Western government officials and analysts did not know these facts. So, what was going on? Why did they persist in the charade of making empty pledges to the Palestinians about something they knew could not happen in the conditions as given? While knowing that neither the US president nor a single European leader was prepared to face Israel down, or bring the slightest pressure on it to cooperate? Was this some kind of cynical game to pacify Arab and Muslim opinion and maintain a liberal peace-loving façade for their own electorates?

If the West was playing a game, then it was a deadly one, played at the expense of Palestinian lives and the stability and security of a whole region. Indulging Israel's adventurism and intransigence had led to this impasse. Continuing the practice would be an act of criminal negligence and unforgivable irresponsibility. The Palestinians and the rest of the Arabs were entitled to know if the West was serious about a proper settlement to the conflict, or if it was playing games. If the former, then it would have to take the necessary steps to bring that settlement about. If there was any possibility that it was the latter, then the Palestinians would have to withdraw from a peace process set up on such terms. For far too long, as it was, they had allowed themselves to be used as pawns in a game played for other people's ends, be they Zionists fulfilling their dreams, Europeans expiating their post-Nazi guilt, Americans implementing their strategic aims and expressing their evangelical fervour, and Arab regimes legitimising their existence to their populations. Had the Palestinians appreciated their own strength – as potential de-stabilisers in an important region, as global icons for millions of oppressed people, as the key to defusing anti-Western Islamic rebellion and as the lynchpin of a peaceful resolution of the Arab-Israeli conflict – they would not have become so subservient to Israeli/ Western designs.

With the Western world intent on keeping Israel happy, what sort of settlement could emerge from such a basis? And if the ongoing sham pretence of a 'peace process' were finally thrown aside, what would be the parameters of a durable and just settlement – not just a short-term political fix, which was all that had ever been on offer?

CHAPTER FIVE

The One-State Solution

The Palestine–Israel conflict has traditionally been presented in the West, especially by Zionist commentators, as extremely complicated. Views predicated on this premise have served not only to obscure the actual situation, but have also forcibly led to the conclusion that the solution to such a problem was bound to be no less complex and probably impossible to achieve. In reality, nothing was further from the truth. The issue is in essence quite simple: a European settler movement ineluctably displaced an indigenous population and wilfully denied its basic rights, inevitably provoking resistance and recurrent strife.

The obvious way to end that strife would have been to redress the injustice done to the indigenous people as far as practically possible, and find a reasonable accommodation for the needs and rights of everyone involved. The parameters of such a solution are clear, and the only difficulty was how to implement them, not because of their complexity, but because of Israel's obdurate clinging to its settler colonialist ideology, Zionism, and the Western support that allowed or even encouraged it to do so.

This chapter is concerned with the question of what constitutes a durable and just settlement between Palestinians and Israelis, irrespective of how attainable it was at the time of writing. The fact that something is right or wrong is independent of what can be done about it. Israel had no new ideas for solving the conflict, only re-workings of the old Zionist formula for maintaining a Jewish state, that is, one with a Jewish majority. In three-quarters of a century, Israel never managed to resolve its original dilemma with the Palestinian presence. Its attempts at obliterating the Palestinians in myriad ways – from their original dispersion, to the denial of their history and existence, to their political marginalisation, to their imprisonment in ghettos – had failed to eradicate them as a physical and political reality.

Yet the Israeli fantasy persisted that it was still possible to pursue a policy against the Palestinians that would simply make the problem go away. This can be summed up as a 'more of the same' strategy: nullifying Palestinian resistance by overwhelming force, confining the Palestinians in small, isolated enclaves so as to prevent their forming any sort of meaningful state, strangling their economy and society, and thus pushing them to emigrate (to Jordan or anywhere else, as long as it was outside what Israel considered to be its borders), and ignoring the rest – the refugees in camps, the other dislocated Palestinians, and those treated as unequal citizens of Israel. The difficulties of managing such scattered Palestinian groupings in order to ensure that none of them bothered Israel would have been a daunting prospect for anyone. But it seemed not to have deterred successive Israeli leaders from trying to make it happen.

The alternative – accepting the Palestinian presence as a reality that had to be addressed through genuine negotiations and a mutually agreed settlement – was not one that Israel wanted to contemplate. The desire on the part of ordinary Israelis for 'peace' was widespread after the Oslo Accords, but it was not accompanied by an acceptance (or even an understanding) of the requirements that such a peace would demand from them. Most of those who accepted the need for Palestinians to have their own state were unclear about the

Palestinian state's exact geography, and unprepared to relinquish land they had come to regard as theirs. In fact, as the Israeli commentator Gideon Levy pointed out in *Haaretz* (19 March 2006), had Israelis seriously supported the creation of a Palestinian state, they would soon have realised that it was not compatible with the carve-up of the West Bank they and their government had brought about. He identified this situation as 'Israel's national disease, to have their cake and eat it'.

Reconciling these opposites had been a central preoccupation of Israeli leaders ever since the acquisition of the 1967 territories and the emergence of the two-state proposition. Israel had been able to ignore this solution for decades until it gathered such inexorable momentum over time as to make it impossible to reverse. Moreover, by its relentless policy of settling Jews in the Palestinian territories (140 settlements dotted all over the West Bank and East Jerusalem, with 100 illegal outposts in 2021), Israel was helping to bring about a situation it desired even less: the inextricable mixing of the two peoples so as to preclude their future separation.

Israeli fears of Palestinians as a 'demographic threat', openly discussed by Israeli politicians and leading figures, were regarded uncritically in the West as legitimate, as if it were acceptable for a nation to define itself exclusively by reference to ethnicity or religion, and seek to exclude those who did not qualify on those counts. It was such ideas of course that had led to the expulsion of the non-Jewish (Palestinian) population from the country in the first place, and which continued to fuel the impetus to expel even more, including those who are citizens of the state. Meanwhile, the Arabs of the West Bank and Gaza were segregated inside their own areas. These Israeli attitudes clearly reflected a combination of the anti-Arab racism that was an inevitable concomitant of Zionism and a feature of the Jewish state from the beginning, and the more recent Israeli fear of 'terrorism' – that is, resistance – for which the mass disappearance of Arabs was seen as the only remedy.

Accordingly, ambitious scenarios for a future Israel, shorn of its Palestinians and safe for Zionism, were much discussed at one time. 'Our future in 2020', published in 2005, envisaged a demilitarised Palestinian state possibly federated with Jordan, with the right of refugee return abrogated, and full normalisation with the Arab and Islamic states. Joint Israeli/Arab projects would be dominated by Israel with the Arabs providing the land and the manpower; the Arab trade boycott would be terminated, and Israel would become the local agent for multinational companies in all parts of the region.[1] A year later, Giora Eiland, a former head of Israel's National Security Council, who did not believe that a Palestinian state in the 1967 territories was viable and might become unstable for that reason, proposed several grand measures to enhance Israel's future security. According to these, Israel would annex 12 per cent of the West Bank and ask Jordan to donate 100 sq. km of its own land to compensate the Palestinians; 600 sq. km of Northern Sinai would be taken from Egypt and joined on to Gaza to make it more viable, and Egypt could be compensated with 200 sq. km of Israel's Negev Desert. A tunnel would be dug under Israeli territory to connect Egypt with Jordan.[2] Eiland did not explain why either Jordan or Egypt should accept these encroachments on their land and security. Yet in 2022, after nearly two decades, versions of these proposals were still being considered.

The Jordanian option, where the Palestinian enclaves would be formally attached to Jordan, had gone into abeyance following Ariel Sharon's death in 2014. Jordan had always struck Sharon as the natural home for Palestinians, although he realised that Jordan would not be willing to go along with this. He therefore envisaged that, given time, the Palestinian entity created by Israel's fragmentation policy in the West

Bank, would itself agitate for a federation with 'the artificial kingdom', as he called Jordan. He foresaw it as inevitable that the West Bank Palestinians would meld socially and economically with Jordan (where approximately 60–70 per cent of the population was Palestinian), and together they would form the 'Palestinian state'. The advantage of this outcome for Israel was that the transition would happen peaceably and not appear to have been imposed by force, Amman might replace Jerusalem as the capital of the Palestinian state, and the refugee problem could be solved there. In other words, the Israeli plan was to promote this solution by knowingly creating a fragmented, non-viable entity in the West Bank which was bound to look towards its Jordanian neighbour for a solution.

This plan was not as fanciful as it sounded. Many exiled Palestinians living in Western countries owned second homes in Jordan, went there regularly to see friends and relatives, arranged for local marriages for their children, and aimed to retire there. Since a considerable number held Jordanian nationality – a leftover from the days when the West Bank was annexed to Jordan – it made those moves all the easier. One could see how plausible, even natural, it seemed for the Jordanian state to become the substitute homeland for Palestinians denied any other.

The intense striving for an independent Palestinian state post-Oslo, however, put the Jordanian option out of mind. But it did not vanish from Israel's political thinking. Meanwhile, Israel's only strategy for Palestinians was repression and more repression. Undoubtedly, many Israelis were genuinely afraid of Palestinians, especially after the Second Intifada, and hence their support for the building of the separation wall. But at bottom, there was also the ever-present fear that whatever acknowledgement was made of the Palestinians as a political presence, even a denuded one, could signify the beginning of an unstoppable unravelling of the Jewish state itself.

As ever, the real problem lay with Israel's governing ethos and its inability to evolve. Zionism, which had been so resourceful in its early stages, ingeniously exploiting every opportunity to further its aims and intelligently considering its every move, showed itself in the end to be unimaginative and unable to adapt to new realities. The 'Iron Wall' philosophy of Vladimir Jabotinsky, articulated in the early decades of the twentieth century, remained more than eighty years later Israel's only answer to the problem.[3] To deal with the Palestinian threat by building a wall, both physical and political, that would shut the Palestinians out was the only solution Israel could think of to forestall the inevitable consequences of its project. Basing Zionism inside another people's land without ensuring their effective annihilation, on the model of what happened, for example, in the settler colonialisms of Australia or the US, was a foolish mistake. This omission returns us to Benny Morris's regret, set out at the beginning of this book, that Israel did not expel the whole of the Palestinian population in 1948 and safeguard Zionism's long-term future.

But this did not happen and Israel should have evolved ways over the decades of its existence to address the problem it had created other than by recourse to crude strategies of repression and brute force. Where the global trend was towards pluralism and the integration of minorities, Israel's struggle for ethnic purity was regressive and counter-historical. Nor was it likely that such strategies would work even on the practical level, for, as already discussed, the difficulties of removing so many Palestinians and ensuring that they did not return or resist the fate Israel had assigned to them, were formidable. Pursuing the same 'iron fist' policy Israel had always adopted actually limited its options in the long run. The more Israel repressed the Palestinians, the harder they resisted. Gaza was a case in point where constant bombing and policing was militarily costly, and had not succeeded in quelling its Hamas and Islamic Jihad leadership.

The dead-end route that Israel's ideology had condemned it to is eloquently described in a 2006 *Haaretz* piece by Amir Oren, 'Living by the sword, for all time'.[4] Referring to a recent Israeli Army assessment of the conflict which concluded that it was 'irresolvable', he wrote, 'This is our life (and our death) as far as the eye can see. Endless bloodletting until the end of time.' While Israel clung to a Zionism that precluded any relationship with the Arabs other than one of master and slave, no comfortable outcome for Palestinians, Arabs, or Israelis themselves was possible.

Towards the one-state solution

The twenty-first century is in its third decade, at the time of writing, and the Palestinian situation could be judged to have deteriorated to its worst point since the *Nakba*. Israel had successfully broken up the Palestinian people into fragmented communities living in different localities and under different conditions. Those under occupation in the post-1967 territories are being subjected to hardships that would have destroyed a less tenacious people; the refugees remain in their UN-supported camps in and around Palestine; millions of other exiles have made homes in various countries around the globe, and the Palestinian citizens of Israel are living anomalous lives amongst their usurpers. What had been an effective leadership in such a fragmented situation is largely defunct. The PLO has dwindled into a semblance of its old self, having been adopted by the ever more discredited PA leadership to give itself legitimacy.

Worst of all, an ever more assertive and powerful Israel, heavily backed by Western states, has been left to wreak all this damage without let or hindrance. It is free to pursue its life-long ambition to erase the physical presence and history of the people it has replaced so effectively as to eventually leave no credible witness to what happened, and no one to cast doubt on its legitimacy.

Yet at the same time, the Palestinians are in the process of attaining a global level of support unprecedented in their history. By the dawn of the twenty-first century, the populations of many of the very countries whose governments held pro-Israel positions, were going in the opposite direction. The Palestinian struggle resonated with many ordinary people, especially younger generations in the West, who saw it as a paradigm for what was natural and just. It became the emblem of anti-colonial struggles and anti-racist protests, like the Black Lives Matter movement in the US, twinned with their own. Britain's second main political party, the Labour Party, under Jeremy Corbyn's leadership from 2015 to 2019 openly espoused the Palestinian cause. Had he gone on to become Britain's prime minister in 2019, the UK government would have placed that cause at the centre of a major European country's foreign policy.

This is not to say that Palestinians had won the battle for public opinion in the West. But there was undoubtedly more sympathy for their cause than at any time previously. This was especially the case in the wake of Israel's massive military attacks on Gaza, Operation Cast Lead in 2008–09, and Operation Protective Edge in 2014. Reporting and TV footage of these ferocious assaults on a besieged people made a significant impact. Israel's unlawful use of white phosphorus in Operation Cast Lead had visible and horrific effects on civilians in Gaza, many children among them, and the vast differential in the death toll on each side told its own story. In the 2008–09 assault, the Palestinian Ministry of Health numbered 1,440 Palestinians dead, as against the Israeli Defence Forces' (IDF) figure of just 13 Israelis. In 2014, the UN estimated at least

2,104 Palestinians had been killed, and 66 Israelis. More than half of the Palestinian casualties were civilians, in contrast to a majority of soldiers on the Israeli side. In the aftermath of the May 2021 uprisings, with Gaza attacked again, international support for Palestinians rose to new heights.

A YouGov opinion poll conducted in Britain, France and the US at the end of Operation Protective Edge in August 2014 reflected the effect of these assaults. Public sympathy for the Palestinians doubled in Britain, and increased in France, though to a lesser extent. It remained unchanged in the US, where support for Israel is traditionally high. But even in the US, a later Gallup poll in 2020 found a modest increase in support for Palestinians among groups previously known to be unsympathetic, that is, older, white Americans, those with some college education, conservatives and moderates.

Other US opinion polls have reinforced this picture. Gallup's World Affairs surveys indicated a more favourable US trend towards Palestinians from 2001 onwards, and a 2016 Pew Research Center survey noted growing support amongst young Americans, up from 9 per cent in 2006 to 27 per cent. None of this seriously dented support for Israel, consistently higher at 50 to 60 per cent, but the increase was significant.

Public opinion worldwide in 2018 was assessed to be overall more sympathetic towards the Palestine cause, and less so towards Israel.[5] The BBC's 2012 poll of 22 countries showed Israel to be near the bottom of those most negatively viewed, only just above Iran, Pakistan and North Korea. These modestly favourable changes in opinion polls should be seen alongside the striking situation on student campuses in Britain, and even more so in the US. Students in both countries were active in solidarity with the Palestinians to such an extent that campuses were seen by some Jewish students as intimidating for them. It became commonplace for Israeli speakers, however distinguished, to face disruption to their lectures by pro-Palestinian students.

As with opinion polls, flare-ups of pro-Palestinian student support tended to occur especially at times of Israeli aggression against Palestinians. Following the 2008–09 assault on Gaza, students at British universities up and down the country, including Oxford, the London School of Economics and the School of Oriental and African Studies (SOAS), staged sit-ins and occupations of university buildings. They called on university leaders to divest from arms companies dealing with Israel, provide free visas for students from Gaza, establish scholarships for Palestinian students, and other supportive acts. By 2015, the Student Union at SOAS was demanding that the university, which had close ties with the Hebrew University in Jerusalem, sever its links with all Israeli institutions. The University and College Union, representing college teachers and staff, was working to help Palestinian students gain UK scholarships

This increasing popular pro-Palestinian support could carry the seeds of a future different to the dismal outlook now envisaged. That possibility will be discussed in the Conclusion of this book.

Support for Palestinian statehood

The positive position on Palestinian statehood in the early twenty-first century appeared quite persuasive, almost a done deal. After 2012, when 138 out of the 193 UN member states recognised 'the State of Palestine', Palestine was granted UN non-member observer status. From there, the new state was able to join a number of international bodies; already a member of the League of Arab States, Palestine became a member of the Organisation of Islamic Cooperation, the International Olympics Committee, the Group of 77 developing nations (of which it was made chair in 2019), and UNESCO. In 2014, the International Criminal Court recognised Palestine as a state, permitting it to bring cases before the Court.

In conformity with UN Security Council Resolution 242, the UN recognised the territory of this state to be 'based on the 1967 borders', with East Jerusalem as its capital. The geographical borders of the new state have never been defined any more exactly than that, and a stipulation that there should be a mutually agreed 'land swap' is just as unclear. According to this, West Bank territory occupied by the Israeli settlements would be annexed to Israel in exchange for equivalent Israeli territory for the Palestinians. But the exact parameters of this land swap were never defined or agreed upon, though it was understood that the area of land exchanged would be between 1 and 3 per cent.

The Palestinian state, which these moves were helping to create in concrete form, is an essential component of the two-state solution. This solution is currently seen as the only realistic option for the future of Israel and the Palestinians. It is approved by the international community, and has no serious competitor except in the wishful thinking of idealists and activists who dream of a single democratic state replacing the present arrangement in Israel-Palestine. President Biden's new administration in 2021 reaffirmed its commitment to the two-state solution, and intended to re-engage the international community through activating the dormant Middle East Quartet.[6] This US determination was strongly reiterated following the uprisings in Israel and the occupied territories during May 2021.

The two-state solution

In 2022, and despite much criticism and disappointment at its lack of success, the two-state solution enjoyed wide international support. A sizeable percentage of Palestinians, especially those under Israeli occupation, also backed this solution, although in decreasing numbers as it became more and more unattainable. For those in the Palestinian diaspora, 'Palestine', after the Oslo Accords had made such a concept possible once again even though so little of it had been liberated, became the focus of their efforts as a place of hope and the potential start of the journey back home.

It is probable that no greater illustration of the triumph of hope over reality exists than the two-state solution. It should be clear to the reader that, given the reality on the ground, there was in 2022 no possibility of a state coming into being that would satisfy the Palestinians' minimal demands. Nor, after 55 years of Israeli occupation, could one envisage a partition of the country as it stood. These facts had been clear for decades, but yet the two-state solution remained on the books at the UN, the League of Arab States, the European Union, the US, the Palestinian Authority, and, as already pointed out, for many Palestinian individuals and communities.

Recognition of the Palestinian state was supposed to be the first step on the way to a lasting resolution. Most Palestinians initially anticipated a growing exchange with Israelis in the context of two neighbouring states at peace, and that this friendly contact would lead in time to a melting of the border between the two and a true mixing of populations. In this way, there could even be a sort of return for the refugees, but not as a way of taking over Israel. Some Palestinians believed strongly that the national quest for an independent state had to be coupled with a genuine and sincere acceptance of Israel's permanence, not a ruse for undermining it.[7]

It was not that these ideas were articulated as such, or even at the forefront of Palestinian preoccupations, in the demand for statehood. The dominant need was to have the occupation lifted and normal life regained, even though it meant dividing what had been Mandatory Palestine into two states, Israeli and Palestinian. This two-state aim is probably the best known and most internationally accepted solution of all for the conflict. Its support amongst Palestinians did not stem initially from any belief that it was in itself an ideal or even a desirable solution, but rather that it was the *only* way, as they saw it, of saving what little was left of Palestine, a place in which to recoup Palestinian national identity and social integrity.

Israel's ghettoisation of Palestinian society had led to a social fragmentation and national disorientation that could only be reconstituted in a Palestinian state free of Israeli interference. Many Palestinians believed that without this crucial phase of healing and reintegration, there could be no advance for the national cause. In addition, and given the massive power imbalance on the one hand and the international support for the creation of a Palestinian state on the other, the two-state solution acquired a 'most we can hope for' character that was indisputable. The fact that for a while it also looked to be potentially attainable added to its attraction.

The Oslo Accords had nurtured in Palestinians both inside and outside the occupied territories an aspiration to statehood, encouraged by Western-funded 'state-building' projects, no less staunch than that which had animated the first Zionists (and with far greater legitimacy). In fact, many wealthy Palestinians consciously emulated the Zionist model by zealously investing in the Palestinian towns Israel had vacated after the Oslo Agreement in order to build their state by incremental steps (though, as they said, without displacing anyone in the

process). Prominent among these was the Palestinian entre-
preneur, Munib al-Masri, whose monumental palace built
commandingly atop a hill in Nablus struck me when I saw it as
a statement of possession meant to defy the Jewish settlements
encroaching on his city, which were all deliberately sited on
hilltops in a crude bid to claim the Arab land below them for
Israel.

Palestinians have always rejected the idea of partition,
although it was a familiar one in Palestine's history as a device
used by Britain and later the UN for accommodating Zionist
ambitions in the country. The Zionists first proposed it to the
Mandate authorities as far back as 1928 when their numbers in
the country were very small.[8] In 1937, the Peel Commission
set up by the British Government to find a solution for the
conflict between Jews and Arabs in Mandate Palestine, recommended that the country be divided into Jewish and Arab
states. In 1947, UN General Assembly Resolution 181 made
the same recommendation and for the same reason. The story
of how this resolution, which the UN was not legally entitled
to table in the first place, was pushed through to a vote in its
favour is an ignoble one.

It is no secret that it took vigorous US and Zionist arm-
twisting and intimidation to overturn the majority of states
that would have voted against it.[9] The resolution was passed
against strong Arab opposition (though some Palestinian
communists accepted it, hoping it would put a brake on Zionist
colonisation), not least because it was the first international
recognition accorded to what was a blatantly unjust, settler
colonialist enterprise in an Arab country, and which the
Zionists used subsequently to legitimise their presence. It
was seen as an extension of the original injustice perpetrated
in 1921 by the League of Nations in conferring on Britain a
mandate to encourage Zionist settler colonialism in the first
place. For the people of Palestine, partition was an outrageous

assault on the integrity of their country and a gift to the Jewish immigrants of a statehood they did not deserve. This remained the Palestinian position after 1948, when the aim of the newly formed PLO in 1964 was Palestine's total liberation, 'the recovery of the usurped homeland in its entirety', as the Preamble to the 1964 Palestine National Charter phrased it.

In 1974, however, the question of partition returned, at least implicitly, to the national agenda. At its twelfth meeting, the Palestine National Council (PNC) formally resolved to set up a 'national, independent and fighting authority on every part of Palestinian land to be liberated' from Israeli occupation. Although there was no mention of a Palestinian state and no recognition of Israel, the resolution paved the way to a new thinking about the future. This was reflected in the next PNC meeting in 1977, which called for 'an independent national state' on the land, without referring to its total liberation. By 1981, the PNC had welcomed a Russian proposal for the establishment of a Palestinian state, and the idea of a two-state solution was becoming increasingly familiar.[10] In 1982, the Saudi-inspired Fez Plan, which called for the creation of a Palestinian state in the occupied territories and an implicit adoption of a two-state solution, also won guarded Palestinian endorsement. Jordan began to feature as the other part of a possible Palestinian/Jordanian confederation in the PNC meetings after 1983. This was accompanied by an increasing emphasis on the attainment of Palestinian goals by diplomatic means, including for the first time an endorsement of ties with 'democratic and progressive' Jewish and Israeli forces and the internationalisation of efforts to find a peaceful solution.

The outbreak of the First Intifada and the PLO's isolation following its expulsion by Israel from Lebanon in 1982 were important factors in accelerating the trend towards the two-state solution. Palestinian awareness of the realpolitik of Israel's power and the futility of military struggle against it convinced the PLO to adopt a political programme that reflected this reality. Hence it was the PLO which came to recognise Israel and propose the creation of an independent Palestinian state alongside it as the aim of the Palestinian struggle. This was a recognition that what was just was a separate issue from what was possible and attainable under the circumstances, and a decision to pursue the latter at the expense of the former.

What would have been just was for the whole of Mandate Palestine to revert to the dispossessed Palestinians, thus solving the refugee problem for good, and for Israel to compensate them for their losses over the years. But the PLO saw this was impossible to realise and so opted for what was, they believed, attainable. At its eighteenth meeting in November 1988, the PNC accepted UN Resolutions 242 and 338 as the basis for negotiations with Israel. It also and most significantly accepted the previously rejected and humiliating UN Partition Resolution 181, finding itself acquiescing 41 years later to the division of Palestine and recognising Israel as a legitimate state. The Declaration of Independence that was the hallmark of this meeting set down the notion of a Palestinian state, implicitly to be established within the 1967-occupied territories, with East Jerusalem as its capital. A month later, the PLO chairman, Yasser Arafat, reinforced this recognition of Israel in an affirmation of 'the right of all parties to the conflict to live in peace and security'.

The PNC was the dispersed Palestinian people's best attempt at a representative body in exile through which to reflect the broad range of their views. Even so, the 1988 decision voted in by the PNC was not uniformly welcomed, and the idea of a 'statelet' on 23 per cent of the original Palestine's territory was met with derision by many individuals and groups. The retreat from the original PLO goal of Palestine's total liberation, which had become evident since 1977, was regarded by this constituency as a craven capitulation to Israeli hegemony. I remember how angry my fellow activists in London felt at this betrayal of principle. They convened meetings, wrote defamatory articles and made speeches denouncing the 'statelet' and demanding a return to the PLO's original charter. The first London PLO representative, Said Hammami, posted there in 1975, strongly supported the creation of a Palestinian state and responded to these accusations with fierce condemnation. I recall him telling me with a chilling prescience he could not have been aware of at the time, 'So, you don't approve of what we [the PLO] are doing? Believe me, the day will come when all of you will rend your clothes with regret you did not fight for the "statelet", because even this small thing will be denied us, you will see!'

After the 1993 Oslo Accords made implicit the goal of creating a Palestinian state, which Palestinians and international agencies started to prepare for in the occupied territories with enthusiasm, the two-state solution dominated the international political discourse, even, as we saw, amongst Israelis. It was affirmed by UN resolutions, at one time formed part of George W. Bush's vision for the future of the region and was central to the 'Road Map', laying out the path to an international peace proposal. Sharing the fate of all other peace proposals for this conflict, however, it was never implemented. Barak Obama's Secretary of State John Kerry made indefatigable peacemaking attempts in 2014 to make the two-state solution a reality, but to no avail. As Obama left office in 2016, he was still trying to work out a way to leave an outline for the two-state solution, possibly through the UN.[11] His successor, Donald Trump, also supported the two-state solution, although in a form so distorted by pro-Israel bias, it was scarcely recognisable as such.[12]

However, in 1993, the international consensus was not *whether* a Palestinian state would be created but *when* and in what territory. The Palestinian doubters went into abeyance, waiting to see what would happen or half-believing that their fears had been misplaced, and the return of Yasser Arafat and the PLO leadership to Palestine seemed to herald a new dawn.

But it was a false dawn. Israel's policy of 'creating facts' on the ground, the single most effective foil to these plans, put the creation of a sovereign, viable Palestinian state out of reach, and thereby spelled the end of the two-state solution. As Israeli colonisation and segmentation of the West Bank proceeded unimpeded throughout the years since 1967, up to and including the period after the Oslo Agreement, the Palestinian territories supposed to form the state were rendered unusable for that purpose by the jigsaw of Jewish colonies, bypass roads and barriers.

Jerusalem was judaised beyond the possibility of its becoming the Palestinian capital, and Gaza was left stranded in an Israeli sea, unconnected to the rest of Palestine, its single shared border with Egypt not under its control. These logistical obstacles in the way of a viable Palestinian state became so extreme over the decades that many observers, including the most ardent supporters of the two-state solution, started to fear that it was not going to happen. The UN Special Rapporteur on the situation of human rights in the Palestinian territories was forced to conclude as far back as 2006 that 'this vision [of a two-state solution] is unattainable without a viable Palestinian territory. The construction of the wall, the expansion of settlements, the de-Palestinisation of Jerusalem and the gradual incorporation of the Jordan Valley are incompatible with the two-state solution.'[13] Numerous studies and commentaries appeared, analysing this problem and drawing the conclusion that a two-state outcome had been superseded.[14] The head of the Israeli Committee Against House Demolitions (ICAHD), Jeff Halper's concept of Israel's occupation as a triple-layered 'matrix of control' – military, territorial and bureaucratic – is probably the most graphic of these and the best illustration of Israel's tenacious and irreversible hold on Jerusalem and the West Bank.[15] The geographer Jan de Jong's maps of the occupied territories vividly demonstrated the impossibility of a Palestinian state arising in these segmented lands.[16]

Given this situation, Palestinian Authority officials indicated that they would be forced to abandon the two-state solution and press for equal citizenship with Israelis.[17] The need to dissolve the PA and force Israel to deal with the Palestinians directly as a people under occupation rather than shielding behind the fiction of an independent government was openly debated.[18] Ahmad Qurei, the Palestinian prime minister at the time, announced in January 2004 that if the two-state solution were made impossible to achieve, then the Palestinians had no alternative but to aim for one state, a tactic meant to 'scare' the Israelis and their US sponsors into checking the growth of settlements and other obstacles to the creation of a Palestinian state. These assertions have been made several times subsequently.

But they scared no one, since Israel had no intention of ever letting a viable Palestinian state come into being. Its colonisation programme and studied avoidance of serious peace agreements or meaningful negotiations were all designed to ensure that nothing other than a truncated entity incapable of becoming anything more would ever exist alongside the Jewish state. Had Israel conceded on this point and a sovereign Palestinian state been created within the whole of the 1967 territories, a period of tranquillity might well have ensued. But sooner or later, the basic issues would re-emerge and call for resolution, namely, the initial dispossession that had led to the loss of most of Palestine and the expulsion of its people. Israel could no more abandon the West Bank settlements to allow for a Palestinian state there than it could leave Tel Aviv. As the left-wing Israeli activist Haim Hanegbi put it, 'Any [Israeli] recognition that the settlements in the West

Bank exist on plundered Palestinian land will cast a threatening shadow over the Jezreel valley and over the moral status of Beit Alfa and Ein Harod [places in Israel pre-1967].'[19]

These issues would not be resolved in a territory comprising only one-fifth of the original Palestine and in the absence of a just solution for the refugees, who could not be absorbed into such a small area. The proposed state was scarcely viable as it was, without a further influx of refugees. But it could form the bridgehead for an eventual refugee return. Israelis knew this as well as any Palestinian, which was why they resisted the creation of a sovereign, viable Palestinian state so fiercely and fought against any affirmation of the Palestinians as a people with a national cause. It was also why they needed almost just as much to set up a non-viable entity they would call a state, as a fig-leaf to satisfy the international community. In reality, it would be both a dustbin for dumping unwanted Palestinians who could threaten Israel's demography, and a way of preserving Zionism.

Israel was not wrong in its apprehensions. Those most anxious to bring about this version of the two-state solution were Israel itself and the Western powers, which wanted to save a project they had unwisely backed from the start and could not now abandon. To these may be added the pro-Western Arab states whose chief concern was a quiet life free from Western pressure to accommodate Israel and the wrath of their own populations for doing so. It was true that, in addition, there had grown amongst many Palestinians a genuine desire for a separate state, feelings nurtured by years of deprivation under occupation and, as we have mentioned, the fear of losing the rest of Palestine if they held out for anything more ambitious.

In recent years, a concern with recouping Palestinian identity and society fractured by Israel's separation and closure policies has added powerfully to the desire for independence. Decades of cruel treatment at the hands of Israel also led to considerable hostility towards Israelis, and a longing to separate from them for good. This antipathy only grew with time, provoked by the siege and recurrent bombing of Gaza.

Those understandable reactions aside, what did the Palestinians really gain from a settlement that left the lion's share of their original homeland and its resources in the hands of a Zionist state that had robbed them of it in the first place? And what of the majority of their people, the millions of refugees and displaced, who had no access to that homeland? Why would anyone assume that such obvious injustice could be forgiven or forgotten? In a research study I carried out in 1999/2000, just before the outbreak of the Second Intifada, I interviewed 42 randomly selected Palestinian Arabs and 50 Jewish Israelis about the conditions for reconciliation between them.[20] These were people who came from various walks of life and, had it been a larger sample, might have been reasonably representative. Some twenty opinion-formers from both sides (academics, politicians, journalists) were also questioned about the same topic. The results predictably showed that the greatest differences of view were over the issues considered basic to the Palestinians: the right of refugee return, Israel's acknowledgement of responsibility for their expulsion and the right to compensation.

A 'historic reconciliation' with Israel, as the Palestinian respondents termed it, would require an Israeli apology and acknowledgement of its responsibility for the *Nakba* and accepting the right of return with compensation as basic conditions. (The Israeli respondents, with a few exceptions, were unwilling to accept any of these terms.) Two-thirds of Palestinians were willing to accept the two-state solution, but only as a stage, and all of them considered the area pre-1967 to be Arab land. Was it possible, therefore, that such people could accept a Palestinian state, even had it been available, as anything other than a first stage to a retrieval of the rest of Palestine? Even if it took decades to accomplish, the return of the whole country had to be their final destination.

The two-state solution and the right of return

The refugee issue is possibly the most cogent argument against a two-state solution. The 5 million refugees and their descendants, living in camps, most but not all run by the UN, since 1948 formed the core of the Palestinian problem. They cherished the memory of the lost homeland and reared their descendants on a detailed knowledge of their towns and villages of origin in the old Palestine. On a visit to Bourj al-Barajneh refugee camp in Beirut in 1998, I was astonished to hear small children, aged 4 and 5, reciting the names of places they called their hometowns in what is now Israel. The children all said they were 'going back' there when they grew up. Listening to them, I was both saddened and awed at the tenacity with which the Palestinians held on to the idea of return, despite decades of exile in the worst of conditions and the apparent hopelessness of their cause.[21] I wondered why they were allowed to indulge their dreams in this way, if it were the case that the international community had no intention of implementing the refugees' right to return.

It is no accident that these camps provided the fighters of the PLO formerly and those of Gaza's Hamas activists latterly. The refugees, representing the bulk of Palestine's displaced population in 1948, also delivered a majority of the workforce that helped to build up the Gulf States from the 1950s onwards, and many went on to become successful entrepreneurs, journalists and other professionals. The prominent former editor of the London-based *al-Quds al-Arabi*, and media commentator frequently cited in these pages, Abdel Bari Atwan, for example, started life in a Gaza refugee camp.

The right of return on which all these displaced people's hopes were pinned was a *cause célèbre* for Palestinians. Had there been no refugees and the Palestinian problem merely one of Israeli occupation, the conflict would have been easier to solve. But the 1948 dispossession was a fundamental part of Palestinian history, the legal backbone of the Palestine cause, and the crucial basis on which the Jewish state was built. Few people in the West appreciated the importance of the right of return for Palestinians, which should have been enforced from the beginning, and it became customary for Western policymakers to view the Palestinian refugees as commodities that could be moved about when required, and not as human beings with needs and desires. The fact that this issue was of core importance to Palestinians was constantly ignored. But if there were to be a settlement, the refugee issue would reassert itself forcefully for all Palestinians, and a deal that did not address this would not be considered just, legal, or an end to the conflict.

The two-state solution stood no chance of solving this problem on any count. And strictly speaking, as some have argued, the creation of two states in itself logically ruled out a refugee return to the area within the Israeli state.[22] The two-state solution required the Palestinians to recognise Israel *as a Jewish state*, that is, one with a Jewish majority, and therefore incompatible with an influx of non-Jews. That left the putative Palestinian state as the only option, but it could not hope to accommodate the number of returnees, whatever Israel feared, and especially not as the tiny, segmented entity Israel had in mind. Nor was it fair that people expelled from Haifa or Safad should have to make their homes in Ramallah or Jenin. Had the Palestinians, who were aware of all this, been less desperate for a way out of the dire situation of rapid

Israeli encroachment on their land and existence, they would not have accepted a solution that abandoned the refugees to their fate. Their logic in doing this was to live to fight another day, for the basic injustice of the situation would remain and resurface at a later date. None of the convoluted arrangements devised by Israel and the Western powers to dispose of the refugee issue could make Palestinians forget that it was their homes and land that had been usurped by a people who had no right to them and whose self-righteous ownership of a country that was not theirs was a constant affront.

The one-state solution

The obvious alternative to the two-state proposal was the one-state solution. It is important to understand this was not simply a matter of logic, but of a fundamental difference in approach to solving the conflict. The two-state solution and its variants have as their sole object – no matter what the rhetoric about a 'just and comprehensive settlement' – the termination of Israel's occupation and its damaging consequences for Palestinian civil life in the occupied areas. It leaves untouched the issue of the nature of the Israeli state and its dangerous ideology, Zionism.

A whole literature exists that analyses Zionist ideology, its meaning and significance, in ways that have mystified it into a quasi-religion, an identity, and a badge of honour for Jews. Yet, in its application to historic Palestine, Zionism was a simple, practical programme to take the land but not the people. Palestine, denuded of its Arab inhabitants, would become Jewish owned and so attain the Jewish 'ethnic purity' Zionism longed for. These aggressive and racist aims never changed over time, and no matter how much Palestinian land the state of Israel acquired, in Zionist terms, it was still short of the ultimate goal.

In line with this, many Jewish Israelis saw a continuing need to expel Arabs. In 2006, a prominent Israeli leader was publicly calling for such expulsions from the West Bank.[23] Ten years later, a Pew Center survey found (Reuters, 8 March 2016) that nearly half of Jewish Israelis wanted Arabs expelled or transferred; 79 per cent believed that Jewish citizens deserved preferential treatment; and eight out of ten Arabs interviewed complained of 'heavy discrimination' against them by Jewish Israelis.[24] In 2021, the US-based Human Rights Watch released a detailed report of what it called Israel's apartheid practices, whose effect could be construed as a means to make Palestinian life intolerable and thus encourage outward emigration.[25]

At the same time, the Jewish state remained a foreign body in the Arab region, an anomaly no more ready to integrate with its Arab neighbours than it had been in 1948. That is not to say Israel gained no official Arab acceptance in its 75 years of existence. In 1979 and 1994, it signed peace treaties with Egypt and Jordan respectively; and in 2020, its relations were normalised with the United Arab Emirates, Bahrain, Sudan and Morocco. But these formal alliances were based on Israel's superior power and its standing as a conduit to US favour. In no way did these treaties integrate Israel into the Arab region. Israel remained a state committed to a hostile ideology that could only feed continuous conflict.

In its essence, the one-state solution aimed to address these problems by going to the heart of the matter: the existence of Israel as a Zionist state. If it was the case that the imposition of Zionism on the Arabs had been the cause of the Palestinians' dispossession, the rejection of their rights and the constant state of conflict between Israel and its neighbours, it made no sense for a peace agreement to preserve that status quo. The key date in the genesis of this conflict was not 1967, as the two-state proponents implied, but 1948. Israel's occupation of the 1967 territories was a symptom of the disease, not its cause.

The problem was that the two-state solution did not just confine itself to dealing with the symptoms; it actively helped to maintain the cause. The roots of the conflict, as has frequently been reiterated in this book, lay in a flawed and destructive project that never changed. It refused to adapt to its environment or accept any limitations on its aspirations. Indeed Israel's very success encouraged this process: the more it took and escaped retribution, the more it wanted to take, and so on in a self-perpetuating cycle of aggression and expansionism. Only by bringing the Zionist project to an end, proponents of the one-state solution argued, would the conflict also be ended. Such an approach was a radical challenge to decades of Arab 'pacification' and coercion at the hands of those concerned to preserve the Zionist project.

The one-state solution meant the creation of a single entity of Israel/Palestine in which the two peoples would live together without borders or partitions. An equitable division of a small country like Palestine with resources that respect no borders, especially not artificially constructed ones, was logistically unworkable. All the partition proposals previously devised had discriminated heavily in Israel's favour. The one-state solution was unique in addressing this and all the other basic issues that perpetuated the conflict – land, resources, settlements, Jerusalem and refugees – within an equitable framework. As such, it answered to the needs of common sense and justice, the *sine qua non* of any durable peace settlement.

According to the adherents of the one-state solution, in a single state, no Jewish settler would have to move and no Palestinian would be under occupation. The country's scarce resources could be shared without Israel stealing Palestinian land and water, or Palestinians left starving and thirsty. Jerusalem would be a city for both peoples, not the preserve of Israel to the anger of Arabs, Muslims and Christians, and the detriment of international law. Palestinian refugees would be allowed to return to their original homeland, if not to their actual homes. Their long exile and blighted existence would end, and the states that had played host to them could be relieved at last of a burden they had carried for more than seventy years. The long-running sore of dispossession that had embittered generations of Palestinians and perpetuated their resistance could heal at last.

With the outstanding issues thus resolved, no cause for conflict between the two sides would remain, and the Arab states could then accommodate the Israeli presence in their midst with genuine acceptance. Such an outcome would by extension also dampen down the rage against Israelis and Jews that had come to fuel violence and terrorism. Arab hostility, real or imagined, which Israelis constantly faced and which forced them to maintain their state by superior force of arms and US patronage would end. Israel, which had become the most unsafe place on earth for Jews, could, when transmuted into the new, shared state, be a place of real refuge for them. A normal immigration policy, once the returning Palestinian refugees had been accommodated, would operate, under which Jews and others who wanted to live in Palestine/Israel could do so according to fair and agreed rules.

On this analysis, the one-state solution was the most obvious, direct and logical route to ending an intractable conflict that had destroyed the lives of so many people and damaged the Middle East region so profoundly. And for that reason it should have been the most actively pursued of all the options, but especially by the Palestinians, for whom it meant a reversal (as far as that was practically possible) of a process that had robbed them of their land and made them stateless refugees.

People often discussed the one-state solution as if it were a revolutionary idea. But it was no forward-looking innovation:

rather more a way of going back, of restoring a land deformed by a near-century of division, colonisation and plunder to the whole country it had been before 1948. It was a healthy rejection of disunity in favour of unity and a humane desire for a life based on cooperation rather than confrontation. How much better for Israeli Jews to learn to live together with Palestinian Arabs in a relationship of friendship and collaboration that had the potential to be excitingly productive, rather than be condemned to the barren and dangerous dead-end future that Israel was driving them towards.

Variations on the one-state theme

In spite of the obvious advantages of a one-state solution, its very mention was traditionally met with a variety of objections, the most cogent (and accurate) of which was that Israel would never agree to it and thus it was dead in the water before it started. In fact, the idea of Arabs and Jews sharing their land had a long and notable pedigree, far longer than that of the two-state solution, which was a recent notion in Palestinian history arrived at, as we saw, in response to a series of defeats for the Palestinian national liberation movement. There were two main ways in which Palestine could be shared: the bi-national model in which the two groups could share the country but remain ethnically separate, and the secular democratic, one-person-one-vote model, based on individual citizenship and equal rights irrespective of race, religion, or gender. The bi-national model preserved the structure of the two religious/ethnic communities, while the secular democratic model emphasised the individual rather than the community, in the style of Western liberal democracies. Thus bi-nationalism enabled Zionism to survive, albeit in a reduced form, while the secular democratic alternative did not.

The bi-national state

The various ideas for partition which were put forward during the Mandate period were really bi-nationalist proposals that answered to the Zionist need to separate from non-Jews in a space which would permit a Jewish majority to exist. Their aim was the revival of Jewish life in its 'ancestral homeland', as they phrased it, which should not be incompatible with Arab life in the same space.

Judah Magnes was the strongest proponent of this 'cultural Zionism'. His vision was of a bi-national state as part of a wider federation with the Arabs states, whereby Jewish immigration would not lead to Palestinian dispossession.[26] Such ideas led to the formation of the Brit Shalom organisation in 1925, which proposed adopting the Swiss or Finnish bi-national models for a putative shared state with the Arabs. Magnes later impressed the Anglo-American Committee of Inquiry, set up in 1946 to investigate post-war Jewish immigration to Palestine, with these bi-nationalist ideas. With his fellow members of Ihud (Hebrew for 'union'), the organisation he founded to promote bi-nationalism, he went on to testify to the UN on the same subject.[27]

David Ben-Gurion, while chairman of the Jewish Agency in 1930, thought that a balance between Arabs and Jews in a bi-national state was necessary in order to guard against the danger of one side ruling the other. Mapai, the main Zionist party of the time, adopted this view in 1931. Indeed, between 1921 and 1939, the Zionist leadership, which included Chaim Weizmann, tended to be somewhat bi-nationalist in orientation.[28] The socialist-Zionist organisation, Hashomer Hatzair, founded in 1946, also advocated bi-nationalism as the means to realise the aims of Zionism.

For the Zionists, who were simply an immigrant minority, sharing the country would have been quite an achievement. Their support of bi-nationalism, which would have brought them closer to their goal, was mainly based on that consideration. Needless to say, the vast majority of Palestinians felt differently. They did not share these bi-nationalist ideas, which they saw as a means of forcing them to accept that a group of foreign colonists had equal rights with them in their own land.

But during the Mandate years, when Zionists were actively putting these bi-nationalist ideas forward, a very small number of Palestinians did respond positively. Secret negotiations between these Palestinians and the Jewish bi-nationalists took place, negotiations which would have been a source of intense shame to the Palestinians had they been discovered. The Arab bi-nationalists were motivated by a variety of reasons, not all of them noble, for example, accepting bribes in return for their support for Jewish Zionists, or because of internal rivalries between prominent Palestinian families in which supporting the Zionists was used as a weapon in the contest. But a small number of them genuinely believed that the Jewish presence in Palestine could be beneficial by drawing in foreign capital to develop the country. It may also have been their sense that Zionism would prove difficult to dislodge and opted for the best arrangement in such circumstances.

One of these negotiators was Ahmad Khalidi, head of the Government Arab school during the Mandate period; in 1933, he proposed a state divided into two cantons, Jewish and Arab, the latter to be linked to Transjordan, with Jerusalem, Hebron and Safad left outside the cantons as 'free cities' belonging to neither. The cantons would have a joint ruling council of Arabs, Jews and British representatives, and Jewish immigration would be confined to the Jewish cantons and the three free cities.[29] Another adherent was Musa Alami, a member of a prominent Palestinian family and Arab secretary to the British High Commissioner, who also proposed a cantonal plan in the 1930s. The Jewish canton would include the Jewish colonies already established, and a national government with proportional representation would be set up which, inter alia, would restrict immigration to the Jewish canton. During the 1970s, I met Alami in London; he was an old man but still active in running an agricultural project for Palestinian farmers in the West Bank. I found him an impressive figure, despite his age, with sad eyes and a warm, intimate manner. Our meeting was short and the conversation inconsequential, and afterwards I wished passionately that I had asked him to share with me his memories of that special and crucial time in our unrecoverable history.

Fawzi Husseini, the head of the Filastin al-Jadida (The New Palestine) organisation that supported bi-nationalism, was another Palestinian figure who believed that Jews and Arabs could develop the country together as a bi-national state. He went so far as to sign a formal agreement in 1946 with the League for Jewish-Arab Rapprochement and Co-operation, a coalition of several Zionist organisations that sought to build a programme for a bi-national state in Palestine. At the popular level, Palestinian villagers were in neighbourly contact with Jewish settlements in their vicinity and often had friendly relations with them. However, shortly thereafter, fellow Palestinians assassinated Husseini for his pains, and the Zionists rejected the cantonal plans of his predecessors.

Two years later, none of it mattered much anyway, as most of Palestine's indigenous population was expelled and the Jewish state acquired the Jewish majority it had sought. We will never know if the Jewish bi-nationalists would have succeeded in the end, but it is unlikely. They were never anything more than a minority phenomenon and their basic aim was still to establish a European Jewish settler community in an

Arab land, in the belief that the indigenous population could come to accept or even be grateful for it. That such men as Magnes and Buber had the foresight – and decency – to appreciate that the Arab majority in Palestine had legitimate rights and could not be disposed of cannot be denied, and they were often held up as models of virtue. But it did not alter the fact of their unshakeable belief that European Jews like themselves had an equal right to the land of Palestine. Reading this history evokes for me memories of the European Jews I grew up with in Golders Green, a North London suburb with a large Jewish community, who seemed as alien to my native land as, say, the Chinese. The idea that the forebears of such people thought they belonged in Palestine during the 1920s when the country was overwhelmingly Arab and the Jewish state no more than a gleam in Chaim Weizmann's eye, must have struck my forebears as wholly preposterous.

Later bi-nationalism

The bi-nationalist idea became obsolete for decades as the Arab nationalists strove, at lease initially, to reclaim the whole of Palestine, including the territory of the Jewish state. But by the 1970s and 1980s, experiences of the difficulties in integrating ethnic groups harmoniously in one state were also not encouraging to the bi-nationalist model. The conflict in Cyprus between Greeks and Turks, and the struggle for Kurdish independence in Iraq, were frequently cited as examples of the failure of this approach. But in Palestine, bi-nationalism resurfaced in the last years of the twentieth century, as the pre-1948 problem of having to accommodate two communities living in the same space returned. Thanks to Israel's colonisation of the West Bank and Gaza, the two peoples became inextricably mixed, making partition an impossibility and evoking the question of bi-nationalism once again. In fact, some observers argued that the Oslo Agreement itself was a bi-nationalist arrangement because it set up a division of responsibility based on ethnicity between the Palestinians and the (dominant) Israeli groups.[30]

Impelled by the situation of ethnic separateness yet physical connectedness, a small number of Israelis and Palestinians began to discuss the bi-national idea in the 1990s as the only way for the two peoples to share a state and yet preserve their ethnic/cultural identities. This was of great importance to Jewish Israelis of course, but Palestinians also, aware of the need to reconstitute their society and identity, wanted to keep themselves apart for this purpose. Proponents of this solution argued that the two peoples had too strong a national affiliation and self-identification to accept any plan that ignored this important issue.[31] In a bi-national state, each community would be autonomous in terms of language, education and cultural life, and would have its own administrative council to run such affairs. But for matters of common concern, such as national policy, defence and the economy, there would be joint institutions and a joint parliament with equal representation.

By the late 1990s, an active debate on the one-state solution was taking shape, with writers and political figures such as Haim Hanegbi, Meron Benvenisti, Azmi Bishara and Edward Said arguing for such an outcome.[32] (Said's position on this issue was in fact vague. His main concern was the coexistence on humanist grounds between Jews and Arabs in a shared homeland, without spelling out the mechanism that would achieve this.[33]) Long before that, in the aftermath of the 1967 war, the American political scientist, Dom Peretz, had argued for a bi-national state as the preferred solution to the conflict.[34] He saw a Palestine-Jordan federation as a natural part of the plan, with this initial federation later becoming federated with Israel, an idea echoed in the 1971 Jordanian proposal for a 'United Kingdom' of Jordan and the West Bank, and the post-

Camp David confederation or 'condominium' proposals of Menachem Begin and Jordan's King Hussein in the late 1970s. Although the arrangement Israel and Jordan envisaged was for shared rule between them over the occupied Palestinian territories, such a suggestion hinted at the same idea of a Palestine-Jordan federation, whether consciously or not.[35]

The prominent US intellectual Noam Chomsky had been a committed bi-nationalist before 1948. An opponent of the Jewish state as an entity, which could not be democratic and was bound to discriminate against non-Jews, he saw bi-nationalism as the only model for Arab-Jewish coexistence. However, the Jewish state having been established, Chomsky went on to believe that after 1967 there was still an opportunity to create a federal arrangement between Israel and the Palestinian territories, which could make a closer integration between them possible over time. He thought this was a feasible idea up until the 1973 war, when the two-state solution became the adopted international position.[36] In the late 1980s, Sari Nusseibeh, (later the president of Al-Quds University in Jerusalem) put forward the idea of a bi-national Jerusalem by encouraging Palestinian residents to apply for Israeli citizenship. This brought him much opprobrium from Palestinians at the time, although in fact he mainly supported the two-state solution.[37] But a similar equal rights proposal – this time for all the Palestinians under occupation to become Israeli citizens – emerged later, and is discussed below.

Types of bi-national state

The following remarks are meant in no way to provide an exhaustive analysis of bi-nationalism, which is available in many studies elsewhere. A bi-national state could be configured as cantonal, federal, or, in an innovative variation latterly devised by the Swedish diplomat Mathias Mossberg, as 'dual states' superimposed on one another. An earlier writer had proposed a similar idea described as 'parallel sovereignty' for the two peoples in the same territory.[38] These suggestions explored the possibility of Palestinians and Israelis sharing the same land by separating the concept of statehood from territory. Instead of two states alongside each other, Israelis and Palestinians would live in states superimposed on each other. Both of them would have the right to settle the whole area between the Mediterranean Sea and the Jordan River as citizens of each state. But they also had the right to take the citizenship of each other's states if they so wished. Predominantly Jewish localities would belong to 'Israel' and Palestinian ones to 'Palestine', but Palestinian individuals living in an Israeli canton could opt to remain citizens of Palestine and vice versa. Each state would have its own administration and could maintain its separate ethnicity and culture. But there would be a common currency, taxation, labour market, joint defence and other shared services. In essence, this arrangement was similar to the Swiss cantonal system, and could become a truly globalised state of the twenty-first century, where people did not need to be tied to a specific land for national definition.

Lama Abu-Odeh saw the bi-national state as a federation of separate Jewish and Arab administrative units linked to a central government on the US model, as did Tarif Abboushi.[39] The units would be autonomous and could even develop their own economic strategies with help from the central government. Citizens would have the right to move about freely and live in the units of their choice. Since all were supposed to be equal in such a state, resources would need to be transferred from the wealthier (Jewish) units to the poorer (Arab) ones to equalise their status. Such a transfer of funds could also serve as a way for Israel to make amends for the dispossession and exile it had caused generations of Palestinians. The refugees would have the choice of returning to either the Palestinian or Israeli units, or be compensated for their losses and injuries over decades of dispossession.

Nasser Abufarha proposed a bi-national configuration of two sovereign states in political and economic union.[40] The geography of these states would be based on demography: the Palestinian state to include areas of predominant Palestinian habitation, such as the West Bank, Gaza and the Galilee, and the Israeli state those, like Tel Aviv, Safad and Haifa, of predominant Israeli residence. The sparsely populated areas would be part of 'Palestine', reserved for the returning refugees. Each state would have its own legislative council but would be federal in terms of political representation, external security and the economy. The residents of each state would be subject to that state's jurisdiction, regardless of ethnicity. Jerusalem would become a separate district to encompass Bethlehem and would have its own independent council, which would grant equal residency rights to Israelis and Palestinians.

Several other federal solutions were proposed, all based on the concept of two territorially separate states, but without always delineating their exact borders. Belgium, Canada and Switzerland were frequently cited as models. The last was probably the most successful example of how ethnic communities could live peacefully with each other. All 26 Swiss cantons are self-governing, using their own languages and relating to the federal government only in such matters as the judiciary, managing the currency, foreign policy and national defence. In Canada's case, the French and English-speaking divide was managed by granting French-speaking Quebec virtual independence within the federal framework, and Belgium was another example of a federal union between its Dutch and French-speaking halves. This united Flemish and Walloon communities, who were different culturally and had a long-standing history of conflict with each other, and thus made Belgium seem a suitable model for a federated Israel/ Palestine.[41] Its three regions – Flemish, Walloon and that of the capital, Brussels – had their own parliaments, languages and cultures, but citizens could travel and work anywhere in the country. Each ethnic community was responsible for the educational and cultural affairs of its members wherever they resided, so as to maintain a communal cultural continuity outside of geographical space. In a similarly federated Israel/ Palestine, Jerusalem would be the equivalent of Brussels. The federal constitution would protect the rights of Israelis and Palestinians, guarantee religious freedom and separation of church and state so as to guard against Jewish and Islamic theocratic extremism. Returning refugees could live in Israel as well as Palestine, but retain Palestinian citizenship.

One writer looked to the past for ideas, rediscovering the UN Special Committee on Palestine's (UNSCOP) bi-national proposal of 1947 as a model for a modern solution.[42] This proposed the creation of federated Jewish and Arab states with Jerusalem as the common capital. The federal authority would draw up a constitution that guaranteed equal rights for citizens irrespective of race or religion, and was responsible for defence, immigration, foreign policy, currency and taxation. Another model was the Malaysian multi-ethnic state, which was a successful example of how to resolve years of inter-ethnic strife by intelligent economic and social policies.[43] Numerous other types of federal, confederal and cantonal arrangement, from Argentina to the Russian Federation to Switzerland, each with its own combination of self-rule and central authority, were discussed. Any of these examples could have provided inspiration and possible models for a federated or bi-national Palestine/Israel.[44]

Tamar Hermann has neatly divided the history of the bi-national idea into four stages.[45] First, there was the 'old school' of Jewish bi-nationalists who did not regard this

solution as ideal but as a way of defusing inevitable strife
between the two communities. Second was the 'new school' of
Jewish bi-nationalists: individuals motivated by concern about
the viability of Israel as a Jewish state and who saw this solution
as the only way for saving Israeli Jews from themselves. Third
were their Palestinian bi-nationalist counterparts who sought
a way in the present unfavourable power structure to realise
Palestinian national rights. And fourth were the advocates
of bi-nationalism and secular democracy from the outside,
affected, in Hermann's view, by their experience of living under
multicultural Western democracies and wishing naively to
apply the same model to the situation in Israel/Palestine. None
of these groups thought the bi-national solution desirable, she
judged, but they advocated it because the reality on the ground
precluded both sides from exercising their 'right' to statehood in
the whole of the territory. Finally, there was a motley collection
of intellectuals who were neither practising politicians nor
decision-makers, and hence detached from reality.

The 'democratic non-sectarian state'

The idea of a secular democratic state, or at least its 'non-sectarian' antecedent, originated with the PLO in the late 1960s.
As such, it was the first initiative for a future settlement to
emanate from the Palestinians themselves. Up until then, virtually all bi-nationalist and partition proposals during the
Mandate years came from British or Zionist sources, and
the latter, as we saw, were confined to a small minority. By
contrast, the one-state proposal espoused by the Palestinians
was the position of their formal representative in exile, the
PNC. At its fifth meeting in 1969, it envisaged a liberated Palestine that would be home to all its citizens, to live in a 'free
democratic society encompassing all Palestinians, including
Muslims, Christians and Jews'.[46] Later, 'society' was amended

to 'state' and this 'Democratic State of Palestine' remained the theme of all PNC meetings until 1973. At its meeting that year, it resolved that all citizens would live 'in equality, justice and fraternity', in a state 'opposed to all forms of prejudice on the basis of race, colour and creed'. The international peace agreements put forward during this phase did not accord with this vision, nor did any of them make mention of Palestine's total liberation. Resolution 242 relegated the Palestinian issue to one of a mere 'just settlement for the refugees'; the 1969 Rogers Plan was based on this resolution, and Jordan's 'United Arab Kingdom Plan', which was devised in 1972 and proposed a union between Jordan and an autonomous West Bank state, were all rejected on those grounds.[47]

The idea of a democratic Palestine state ('non-sectarian' was the term actually used, not secular, although in 1970, Yasser Arafat referred to a 'secular state' on one occasion and retracted it soon afterwards), was more than just a slogan for the Palestinians. The PLO aimed to achieve this goal in practice through armed struggle and, after the 1971 PNC, through diplomacy as well. Some PLO factions, notably the PFLP (Popular Front for the Liberation of Palestine) and PDFLP (the Popular Democratic Front for the Liberation of Palestine), thought the way forward was through a popular struggle first to overthrow the pro-Western Arab regimes. Otherwise, these regimes would only foil Palestinian efforts at liberation if they remained in power. (It was this stance that led to the 'Black September' confrontation with Jordan, which proved so costly to the PLO.) But, following the 1973 Arab–Israeli October War, the PLO's position became more pragmatic, as they hoped to reap some reward from a comprehensive Middle East settlement that appeared to be possible in the aftermath of that war.

Although the Palestinian leadership had been considering the idea of setting up a Palestinian state on the West Bank

and Gaza since 1971 – at least as a first step towards total liberation – it was not until the twelfth PNC in 1974 that their
position became official. By dropping the goal of a non-sectarian state for that of a 'National Authority' on any Palestinian
land liberated by the armed struggle, the PNC signalled a fundamental change of direction that was to lead ultimately to the
Oslo Accords. Nevertheless, the democratic one-state option
was never formally renounced as the ultimate aim of the Palestinian Movement until 1988, when the PNC voted for an
independent Palestinian state and recognition of Israel. In the
intervening years, the one-state alternative gradually faded
from the debate and went quietly into abeyance as a noble
dream, or as some Palestinians put it, a 'preferred outcome'
that was unattainable in the circumstances obtaining at the
time (and since).

By proposing the creation of one democratic state in Palestine, the PLO had taken an extraordinarily imaginative leap
to map out a vision that acknowledged the Jewish presence
on equal terms in the Palestinian homeland.[48] That the very
people who had been dispossessed by the Jews should have
devised a solution based on sharing with these Jews, rather
than retaliatory expulsion and revenge, was a major concession
that should have been acknowledged as such and applauded.
Instead, and predictably, Israel rejected it out of hand, arguing
that the Palestine National Charter, which defined the Jews as
those living in Palestine before 'the Zionist invasion' and thus
excluded most of Israel's population, made any accommodation with the Palestinians impossible.[49]

This was a wilful misreading of the change in the Palestinian position, and Israelis, dismissing what was a liberal and
humane approach to the conflict, were at pains to destroy it
and discredit the motives behind it, even asserting that the
one-state proposal was no more than a recipe for committing
genocide against the people of Israel.[50] At the same time, and

for no reason other than that they thought it premature, not one Arab or other country showed any interest in or even discussed the one-state proposal. The Palestinians themselves seem also not to have thought through the implications of such a solution, or to have produced a plan for how it would be implemented. Obvious problems, such as the exact meaning of 'non-sectarian' in practice, or of introducing secularism to a largely religious society, or the issue of accommodating a vibrant and growing Palestinian nationalism, or the difficulties for Palestinians of coexistence with a people who had colonised and usurped their country, were glossed over or not addressed.

In reality, the Palestinian position on the democratic non-sectarian state was more complex than that apparently straightforward designation suggested.[51] The PLO was aware that, as a solution, such a state was most unlikely to be implemented in the short term, and in any case various Palestinian factions and leaders interpreted the concept differently. Most were agreed on the need to define what sort of Palestinian state they were seeking after liberation and that a democratic, non-sectarian state was the ultimate goal, but they differed over its precise meaning. Some leaders spoke of Jews having 'national rights' within such a state and the PDFLP, which promoted this position, was suspected of secretly aiming for a federal or two-state solution. Fateh wanted the state to be linked to the Arab world, something that Israeli Jews would be unlikely to accept, but it also spoke of building a country together with them, in which the two peoples could live together and 'mutually interact'.[52] Other leaders thought a federal arrangement on the Swiss or Czech models might be acceptable. Two PLO factions, the Iraqi-backed Arab Liberation Front and the Syrian-backed al-Sai'qa, by contrast, totally rejected the idea on the grounds that no resolution of the conflict could be independent of wider Arab agreement.

Why did the Palestinian Movement put forward the non-sectarian democratic state proposal? Plausibly it was a way of opening up the debate on what would constitute an egalitarian solution to a conflict where justice was of paramount importance. The right of return was at the forefront of Palestinian preoccupations, especially those members of the diaspora from where the PLO proposal originated, and they thought that this was the only method of making it happen. At the same time, Palestinians recognised that no progress was possible without taking into account the presence of a strong and established Israeli Jewish society in their homeland. But they did not develop the non-sectarian state idea beyond the outline stage, probably because it struck them as futile when the concept itself had not been agreed by Israel or even amongst themselves, and thus getting bogged down over the practical details was pointless.

As Yasser Arafat said at the time, 'We do not debate the structure of the new state in detail because what we need now is the greatest possible national cohesion'.[53] Moreover, for many Palestinians, the unitary state was a theoretical notion they could not identify with and whose nature they were unclear about. The prospect of sharing the country with those who had usurped it and abused them struck them as intolerable. Thus the proposal was never adopted at the popular level, and the internal contradictions and lack of an agreed position amongst the leadership made it even less appealing. It was not followed up, even by its progenitors, and remained for decades as vague and unformed as when it was first proposed.

The secular democratic state: Later developments

The secular, democratic one-state solution did not return to the political debate until the early 1990s, although it continued to inspire a small minority of Palestinian and other left-wing intellectuals.[54] Its later revival was roughly contemporaneous with that of the bi-national alternative, but initially, the Israeli adherents of the secular state were even fewer than those advocating bi-nationalism. And even then their real numbers were obscured by the fact that the advocates of the one-state idea often did not distinguish between that state being bi-nationalist or secular democratic, although the two were fundamentally different. Many Palestinian one-state support-ers, especially those inside the occupied territories, came from the ranks of those who feared that the two-state solution was no longer feasible. This prompted demands for annexation to Israel if its colonisation of Palestinian territory continued to destroy the two-state solution.

We pointed out earlier how Ahmad Qurei, the Palestinian prime minister, had warned of such an outcome in early 2004, but he was also echoing the popular and influential Fateh leader Marwan Barghouti's call, prior to his imprisonment in Israel, for a one-state option for the same reason.[55] In this way, the struggle against occupation would be converted into a demand for civil rights inside an expanded Israeli state, and was the last thing Israel wanted.

The more Israel colonised and fragmented the Palestinian territories, the greater was the number of Palestinians demand-ing a one-state solution. It was even reported in 2003 (*Yediot Ahronot*, 28 November) that a Fateh leader, Qaddura Faris, was setting up a one-state party to promote the proposal for annexation to Israel. Implicit in these moves was an undeclared desire for the demographic issue, so feared by Israel, to play to the Palestinians' benefit through a one-person, one-vote system where their numbers would make a difference. As Gary Sussman commented, Israel's greatest 'weakness' would become the Palestinians' greatest advantage.[56]

Ironically enough, annexation was not just a Palestinian demand. Hardline Israelis also wanted the Palestinian territories joined on to a Greater Israel and proposed giving those Palestinians who refused to leave them 'residency' status, or a form of reduced citizenship as a mechanism for decreasing the Palestinian presence. Effi Eitam, the right-wing Israeli politician who proposed this, wanted no Arabs in Israel at all.[57] Support for the secular state idea came mainly, however, from diaspora Palestinians, those opposed to Zionism, and left-wing intellectuals who decried the principle of ethnic or religious states and had always held those views.[58] South Africa was frequently invoked as a model of a secular state that had made apartheid obsolete, and, by analogy, if such a state were to replace Israel, it could do the same for Zionism. As the Washington-based journalist (and now publisher), Helena Cobban pointed out, Israel would discover, like South Africa before it, that no amount of repression, fencing-off, or military attacks on neighbouring states could bring it peace, and so Israelis might have to settle for a one-person, one-vote unitary state.[59] Similarly using the South African model, the Israeli activist Jeff Halper argued that bi-nationalism was logistically impossible given the physical intermingling of Israelis and Palestinians on the ground.[60] The only alternative, he believed, was a unitary, democratic state and in order to attain such a state, a South Africa-style anti-apartheid struggle against Zionism would be needed. Implicit in this was the acknowledgement that Israel's occupation was irreversible and all that was possible was to try and neutralise its controlling effects. He called for a campaign, not to end the occupation, which was a hopeless task, but for equal rights in a democratic, 'one-person, one-vote' state.

Halper was one of the few people prepared to outline a practical strategy for achieving the goal of the unitary state. Another was the Israeli writer, Daniel Gavron, an ardent

Zionist turned unitary state supporter after the Second Intifada.[61] He saw that the only solution was a sharing of the land between Jews and Arabs, and proposed a schedule for doing this, starting with the annexation of the Palestinian territories to Israel, followed by universal franchise, and then the creation of a multi-ethnic state.

However, the main thrust of the argument of those advocating the one-state solution was still predominantly theoretical, especially amongst Jewish intellectuals like Tony Judt and Daniel Lazare, who did not distinguish between bi-nationalism and its secular democratic alternative in their concern with the failure of Zionism and the Jewish State. Lazare summed up the objections to a state based on 'religio/ethnic policies elevating one group above all others', and hence increasingly abnormal in a modern world that shunned such practices.[62] In a later wide-ranging review of books on Israel and Zionism, he posed the question of whether Zionism was a failed ideology and raised the need for a bi-national solution.[63] The British-Jewish historian Tony Judt had earlier written eloquently of his dismay at the Jewish state, which he saw as 'an anachronism' in a modern multicultural world that emphasised citizenship rather than race, religion, or ethnicity.[64] Israel came into being, he thought, at a time when the idea of nation states was over. He concluded that a two-state solution was inappropriate in such a situation, and the preferred outcome was a unitary, bi-national state. Judt was resoundingly attacked for this view by furious American Jews, who threatened his life and accused him of being a 'self-hating Jew', but it was an indication of the strength of the debate that was developing around the one-state solution after 2000.[65]

A growing debate

A newfound interest in the unitary state became apparent in the wake of the Second Intifada, largely provoked by Israel's

refusal to abandon Palestinian land or respond to Palestinian demands for independence. Concern with the best way
out of the impasse led to the creation of groups and individuals interested in reviving the one-state solution. In Israel,
the Naturei Karta and the ultra-orthodox Satmar groups had
traditionally supported such a solution, and indeed in March
2006, some of them demonstrated in Jerusalem, declaring that
they did not recognise Israel, only the Palestine of 1948.[66] In
another demonstration by ultra-orthodox Jews in New York
in December 2006, thousands protested against the existence
of the state of Israel as a contradiction to the teachings of the
Torah.[67] But the involvement of a wider range of actors was
new. According to the US-based *Jewish Week* (23 November
2003), this 'alarming idea' had taken hold amongst Palestinians, American left-wing circles and student campuses, and
could garner global support.

In 2003, a Swiss-based organisation, the Association of One
Democratic State in Palestine/Israel, was set up by a Palestin-
ian-Swiss lawyer and soon acquired a membership of over 200
Arabs, Jews and others. By 2006, it had held two conferences,
assembled a literature archive and attracted a range of international supporters, amongst them the Jerusalem-based Rabbis
For Peace, which joined in November 2003.[68] In the same year
a second group, the Right of Return Coalition (*Al-Awda*),
active in other pro-Palestinian fields, formally endorsed the
one-state solution at its international conference in Toronto.
A London-based association, the One-State Group, was established in early 2004 and another in Colorado, the Movement
for One-Secular State.

By April 2004, 15 similar groups were operating, some in
Palestine/Israel, but the majority in Europe and America.[69]
They mainly amounted to just email networks of interested
activists, Jewish, Palestinian and others, and, as in the case
of the London group, an internet archive of relevant litera-

ture. They held sporadic meetings and conducted an active and intelligent debate via the internet on all aspects of the bi-national and secular, democratic state. While working in Ramallah in 2005, I found such a group, Israelis and Palestinians, who met to discuss the issue. Their numbers were small, and the Israeli members made regular visits to their Palestinian colleagues in Ramallah, since the latter were mostly prevented from entering Israel. Another group was centred on the Emil Touma Institute in Haifa, based on an initiative from fellow Israeli and Palestinian academics and activists, prominent among whom was the Israeli historian, Ilan Pappe. I was familiar with most of these groups, and the lively discussions they engendered produced valuable insights that developed the one-state concept well beyond the vague formulation of the PLO's non-sectarian state. One of the members of the London group, the American historian Virginia Tilley, went on to publish a book on the one-state solution that reviewed its history and salient features, drawing comparison with the South African experience.[70]

Gradually, the one-state idea entered the mainstream debate, propelled by the discussions of such groups and the writings of a number of intellectuals and opinion formers. In 2004, the US Green Party adopted the principle of the single-state solution at its national convention, leaving the form of the state for the parties themselves to decide, and the Greens still support one state.[71] Hundreds of articles on the subject appeared in various mainstream publications, many of them quoted here, and the one-state idea was no longer the preserve of a fringe minority.[72] In 2004, the former Iranian president, Hashemi Rafsanjani, called for unification between Israel and the Palestinian territories under one government. 'Jews already present', Palestinian residents and refugees living in neighbouring countries should elect this government. He spoke of harmony between Muslims, Christians and

Jews in one land, thus taking a significant departure from the traditional Iranian line of refusing to recognise that Jewish immigrants had any rights at all in the country.[73] The Libyan head of state, Colonel Muammar Gaddafi, also put forward a proposal for one Israel/Palestine in his 'White Book', published in 2003. This document explained the reasoning behind his adoption of the one-state solution: that 'no other concept is capable of resolving the problem.'[74] 'Isratine', his name for the new unitary state, would be home to Israelis and Palestinians, foremost among them the returning refugees. He considered this the only just solution that would allow the two peoples access to a land they both considered to be sacred. Gaddafi presented his idea to other Arab leaders at the Arab League summit in Tunis in 2004, but there was no support for the proposal, prompting him to walk out in anger.[75]

Several opinion polls on the one-state solution demonstrated some support for it amongst Palestinians under occupation. According to the Palestinian Center for Policy and Survey Research, 27 per cent were in favour of one state (although that might have reflected Palestinian anxieties about the impossibility of attaining the two-state alternative). Indeed, a Jerusalem Media and Communication Centre opinion poll had found that in 1999 fewer than 20 per cent of West Bank and Gaza Palestinians and 15 per cent of Jewish Israelis favoured a bi-national solution if the attempt to establish two states failed. A Peace Index poll of Israelis in 2003 found that 73 per cent feared the emergence of a bi-nationalist state, with only 6 per cent in favour.[76]

In the survey of Palestinians and Israelis I conducted in 1999 and 2000, 22 of the 42 Palestinian respondents were willing to share a state with Israelis and 11 wanted this to be a democracy, asserting that 'Jews used to live with us before.' However, 24 wanted a two-state solution, qualified with such comments as 'a first stage', or 'all we can have for now'. When asked explicitly about a secular democratic state, just three were in favour. Only 13 of 50 Israeli Jews on the other hand were willing to share the land, but only in the West Bank and Gaza, (this was before the latter's evacuation by Israel). Nine were willing to share Jerusalem, but just its eastern half.

I thought at the time that subsequent opinion polls could well have found significant shifts in response to the question of one or two states, and possibly greater support for the one state. But a survey published in August 2020 by the Palestine/Israel Pulse, representing the Palestine Centre for Policy and Survey Research and the Tel Aviv University-based Mediation and Conflict Management centre did not fulfil that expectation. It found a roughly equal support for the two-state solution from both sides, 43 and 42 per cent respectively, and equal lack of support for the one-state solution, at 9 per cent of Palestinians, and 10 per cent of Israelis. But by 2021, a Jerusalem Media and Communications Centre poll found that support for the two-state solution amongst Palestinians had fallen to 29 per cent, and support for the bi-national one-state option had risen to 26 per cent.[77]

In 2007, a major conference devoted to the topic was held at London University's School of Oriental and African Studies (SOAS). In its wake, many were hopeful that the one-state project would develop into a larger movement. However, this did not happen, and some of the one-state organisations and groups mentioned above faded away after a few years, although they gave way to new groups. An example of this is the recently formed One Democratic State Campaign, established in Haifa in 2018. This describes itself as a 'Palestinian-led initiative', though it would be more accurate to say that it is the result of the joint efforts of Jewish and Palestinian activists and intellectuals who are Israeli citizens. It aims to become a broad popular movement that will build a democratic state in the whole of historic Palestine. To that end, it has drawn up an ambitious programme of action, which it was pursuing at the time of writing.

Other one-state organisations have aimed to attract international support for the concept beyond the Palestinian/Israeli constituency. The One State Foundation, legally established in the Netherlands, is one of these. Founded by Israelis and Palestinians, it has sought to engage with the international community to raise awareness of the one-state solution, and thereby to change hearts and minds. Some years before that, the Association for One Democratic State, incorporated in Switzerland, and mentioned above, was committed to drawing support from Palestinians, Jews inside and outside Israel, and members of the international community who signed up for the one-state solution. It is not active any more, and most recently the One Democratic State (ODS) group, registered in the UK in 2013, has been organising to support Jews and Palestinians working for the one-state solution. In addition, the ODS aims to disseminate the concept in European countries, as reflected in their membership. The ODS adopted the Munich Declaration, first developed at a one-state conference in Munich in July 2012, as their foundational document.

The Munich Declaration is an important document that brought together earlier ideas on the one-state solution. It emerged with a ten-point programme of the principles on which a unitary state in Palestine-Israel should be based. These included democracy, equal rights for all, and the right of return of all Palestinians exiled in 1948 and their descendants. Even when not attributed, the Declaration has been adopted more or less by all one-state groups since it first appeared.

A growing literature on the one-state solution

Books and articles on this topic have increasingly made it into mainstream political discourse, although it is difficult to assess how influential they have been in changing political opinion. Even so, there is little doubt they have played a part in spreading awareness of the concept amongst intellectuals, journalists and policymakers.

The earliest studies on the one-state solution appeared in the 1940s, and we have a cluster of publications introducing the idea of bi-nationalism as a model for Jewish-Arab coexistence in Palestine. The solution's proponents, as has been pointed out, were a tiny number of Jewish political thinkers, the best known of whom were Judah Magnes and his Ihud (Union) party. In company with his fellow bi-nationalists, Markus Reiner, Lord Samuel, Ernest Simon and Moshe Smilansky, he put the bi-national case before the UN Special Committee on Palestine in 1947.[78] Magnes was an inspirational figure, not least for his promotion of bi-nationalism; his life and thoughts are reviewed in Daniel Kotzin's *Judah L. Magnes: An American Jewish nonconformist* (Syracuse, NY: Syracuse University Press, 2010).

At about the same time, the Jewish Hashomer Hatzair Workers' Party published a memorandum entitled *The Road to Bi-National Independence*, which it prepared for the Anglo-American Committee in 1947. Contemporaneous with this, the League for Jewish-Arab Rapprochement and Cooperation, also sought a bi-national, post-Mandate state (Aharon Cohen, *Israel and the Arab World*, London: W.H. Allen, 1970). These early writings on bi-nationalism have been assembled and discussed in Susan Lee Harris's PhD thesis, published in 1970 as *The Bi-National Idea in Palestine during Mandatory Times* (Haifa: Shikmona Publishing).

Later studies of bi-nationalism, several of which were mentioned above, put forward proposals for shared sovereignty between the two national communities in one state. They include *The Emergence of a Binational Israel: The Second Republic in the Making*, edited by Ilan Peleg and Ofira Seliktar

(Boulder, CO: Westview Press, 1989); Ahmad Katamesh, *Approach to the Single Democratic State: Two Separate and Interlocked Communities* (transl. from Arabic, Ramallah: Munif al-Barghouti Cultural Centre, 2007); Alain Epp Weaver, *Mapping Exile and Return: Palestinian Dispossession and a Political Theory for a Shared Future* (Minneapolis, MN: Fortress Press, 2014). Yoav Peled and John Ehrenberg's collection of essays, *Israel and Palestine: Alternative Perspectives on Statehood* (Lanham, MD: Rowman and Littlefield, 2016), explores different state models for the two peoples. In addition to these books are several articles about the idea of bi-national sharing, some of which have already been cited.

Publications dealing with the single, democratic state, on the model of one-person, one-vote, were a later development, but have become an increasing feature of one-state literature. Virginia Tilley's *The One-State Solution*, cited earlier, is a prominent example of this genre. Tilley takes as her starting point the logistical impossibility, given Israel's settlements on Palestinian land and international reluctance to confront Israel's illegal behaviour, of any outcome other than one state. Two one-state books by Ali Abunimah, the editor of the *Electronic Intifada* website, are other notable examples: *One Country: A Bold Proposal to End the Israeli-Palestinian Impasse* (New York: Metropolitan Books, 2006), and his later, *The Battle for Justice in Palestine: The Case for a Single Democratic State in Palestine* (Chicago, IL: Haymarket Books, 2014).

Joel Kovel's *Overcoming Zionism: Creating a Single Democratic State in Israel/Palestine* (London: Pluto Press, 2007) is a critique of Zionism as 'state-sponsored racism' and makes a compelling case for the one-state solution. In the same year my own *Married to Another Man: Israel's Dilemma in Palestine*, an account of the steps that made the one-state solution inevitable, was also published by Pluto Press. Two books from 2013 take the argument in other directions; the first is Hani

A. Faris (ed.), *The Failure of the Two-state Solution: The Prospects of One State in the Israel-Palestine Conflict* (London: I.B. Tauris), a collection of papers from a conference examining aspects of the one-state solution. The second is *The One-state Condition: Occupation and Democracy in Israel/Palestine,* by two Israeli writers, Ariella Azoulay and Adi Ophir (transl. from Hebrew, Stanford, CA: Stanford University Press). This interesting book deals with what it calls the 'one-state condition', a description of the differential rule Israel has imposed over the populations of the 1967 and 1948 territories. The authors argue that this one-state condition is a prerequisite for advancing the one-state solution.

A decade before that book, the Palestinian human rights activist Mazin Qumsiyeh had published *Sharing the Land of Canaan: Human Rights and the Israeli–Palestinian Struggle* (London: Pluto Press, 2004). This put forward the thesis of a solution based on sharing the land as the best way to fulfil the needs of justice for Jews and Palestinians. More recently, Cherine Hussein's *The Re-emergence of the Single State Solution in Palestine/Israel: Countering an Illusion* (New York: Routledge, 2015) is an academic account of the single state resurgence in Palestine/Israel. It analyses the idea's potential as a counter-hegemonic force against Zionism, and provides a rich academic apparatus and bibliography which will be of use to scholars and researchers.

Most recent of all has been Jeff Halper's book, *Decolonising Israel, Liberating Palestine: Zionism, Settler Colonialism, and the Case for One Democratic State* (London: Pluto Press, 2021). It maps the journey to the one-state solution, arguing that seeing Israel as a settler-colonialist project is essential to creating a single democratic state in Israel-Palestine. He also sets out the aims of the recently formed One Democratic State Campaign mentioned above.

Other sources on the one-state solution may be found as individual essays or chapters in books. For example, in Ilan Pappe's edited collection on *Israel and South Africa: The Many Faces of Apartheid*, (London: Zed Books, 2015); or Susan Akram, Michael Dumper, Michael Lynk and Ian Scobie (eds), *International Law and the Israeli-Palestinian Conflict: A Rights Based Approach to Middle East Peace* (London: Routledge, 2011). Finally, Judith Butler's erudite study of political Zionism, *Parting Ways: Jewishness and the Critique of Zionism* (New York: Columbia University Press, 2012) presents a vision of cohabitation between the two sides towards a one-state solution within the context of bi-nationalism.

The acceptability of the one-state solution

Interesting as this evolution in thinking on the one-state debate has been, it was nevertheless the case that its opponents were vastly more numerous than its supporters. Although the various one-state associations described above indicate how far a concept with few adherents only two decades ago had travelled, these were still small groups with relatively few supporters; they had no links to any government or institution, and none had been adopted by any official body. The majority of Palestinians rejected the one-state option, and even thought it a dangerous idea because it would distract attention from the urgent struggle to end the occupation. Others were either mystified by the one-state idea or scathing about it. The sometime London head of the Palestinian Delegation, Afif Safieh, held such views with great vehemence. 'If you believe in it,' he told me once, putting his fingers to his lips, 'never ever speak of it! It must remain secret until at least we've got our state.' The American-Palestinian political scientist Ibrahim Abu Lughod regarded those of his compatriots who supported the one-state solution with great hostility. 'You people are little better than traitors to our cause', I remember him declaring when the issue came up at an Arab American University Graduates' conference in Jerusalem in 1993. 'You want to turn us into slaves in a second South Africa!'

During my researches amongst Palestinians in Gaza and the West Bank in late 1999 mentioned above, I found much initial puzzlement and scepticism about the question of the unitary state's actual application in practice. 'It won't work,' most people immediately said. But further discussion usually led to greater interest and more readiness to consider it as a possibility. By 2014, however, with Israel's brutal assaults on Gaza in the background, reaction was angry and hostile to any suggestion of sharing with Israelis. At a meeting in London, several young Palestinian men, holding up pictures of bloody children lying dead in Gaza, told me angrily, 'If you want to let the occupiers into your house, that's your choice. But don't speak for the rest of us!'

The Palestinian sociologist Salim Tamari summarised these concerns in a cogent analysis that considered the bi-national option attractive but simplistic, because it ignored the real situation on the ground.[79] He saw that there was no constituency on either side for such a solution; the Israeli state's established institutions and Zionist consciousness, as well as the material advantages its citizens enjoyed from exploiting Palestinian land and resources, would not be given up lightly; and Palestinians would resist the inevitably inferior position of their community within an advanced, Europeanised, industrial state. Nor could one ask them to abandon their struggle for independence and the end of colonial occupation in order to have them struggle anew against hostile Israeli fellow citizens. If there was to be a bi-nationalist arrangement, Tamari concluded, it should be with Jordan.

Jeff Halper reviewed a list of objections, many of which have already been mentioned, in an exhaustive study in 2002.[80]

Israelis and Palestinians saw themselves as national entities that would not easily be accommodated in a common state; they would not give up their competing claims to self-determination, especially since for the Jews that was a basic feature of Zionism. If Palestinians were made to live with Israelis before they were ready – that is, before attaining an equivalent political, economic and social standard with Israelis – they might remain a permanent underclass. Halper later changed his views as a founding member of the One Democratic State Campaign mentioned above.

According to Robert Keeley, a former president of the Middle East Institute in Washington, DC, a one-state outcome was unimaginable while Israel continued to enjoy the unstinting support of the world's only superpower, the US.[81] He also thought that neither the Israeli Jews, who had worked so hard to create a Jewish state defined as one with a Jewish majority, nor the Palestinian Arabs, who had striven for a state of their own in which to rule themselves would relinquish their positions. He concluded somewhat dramatically that the one-state solution was 'a recipe for disaster for Israel, for the Palestinians, for the entire Middle East, and for the whole world'.

Israeli political figures likewise pointed to the futility of seeking a bi-national or one-state solution while there was such distrust and lack of good will between the parties. The late Israeli writer and campaigner, Uri Avnery, thought it was foolish to abandon the fight for Palestinian independence in return for a chimera. In a well-argued essay, he laid out a list of objections to the one-state solution that were hard to refute.[82] The struggle for a two-state solution had already gained the Palestinian movement a territorial base in the homeland, which, with patience and struggle, he argued, could be expanded, 'dunum by dunum', just as in the Zionist case. Bi-nationalism, on the other hand, condemned Palestinians to life as an underclass in a vastly superior Israeli society, not much different from the fate of the 20 per cent disadvantaged Israeli Arabs already living there. For those who dreamed of a South Africa-type solution where Palestinians in a unitary state would be an underclass only to begin with, later to attract worldwide support for their struggle against Israeli apartheid through their demographic dominance, he had few words of comfort. Unlike white South Africans, who were universally disliked and had few friends, Jews commanded the support of the powerful US Jewish community, and they continued to excite Christian sympathy and guilt over the Holocaust. It was the Arabs, not they, who were the world's bogeymen. The gravest objection to the unitary state from an Israeli point of view, however, as Avnery explained, was that it would be a negation of Zionism, an outcome few Israelis were willing to even contemplate. And that doomed it from the outset.

Like Avnery, the PLO Executive Committee member and co-author of the Geneva Initiative, Yasir Abed Rabbo, opposed bi-nationalism on the grounds that Palestinians did not wish to live as second-class citizens in one state. But he did not rule out that, if forced to live in bantustans as a result of Israel's barrier wall, they would demand a single state 'within a decade or two'.[83] At the same time, the PLO's foreign minister and head of Fateh, Farouk Qaddumi, was clear that a two-state solution was only a stage towards a single state to replace Israel, in line, according to him, with the 1974 PLO incremental position on liberating Palestinian land and establishing Palestinian authority over it.[84] Though such bluntness was not the usual line adopted by Palestinian officials, Qaddumi was speaking for a majority of Palestinians. No Palestinian existed who did not harbour within them a yearning for their lost homeland in its entirety and an intention to return to it some day. No Palestinian accepted that the refugees should never be able to go home.

This was also an aspiration for diaspora Palestinians, who, after 1993, saw a real possibility for the first time of a return in the context of a two-state arrangement with open borders, that could lead to what would effectively be a common state with Israel.

Bi-nationalist, or secular democratic?

The distinction between bi-nationalism and secular democracy is an important one, even though it has often been blurred in one-state discussions. The bi-nationalist solution permitted a degree of communal autonomy and identity but also of separation. In that sense, it was another way of preserving for Jewish Israelis the concept upon which the whole Zionist enterprise was founded: the self-definition of a group by recourse to a questionable religio/ethnic identity that entitled it to a specific territory. It maintained the Zionist myth, that Palestinians did not accept and had fought hard to dispel, of a distinct ethnic Jewish community, which straddled borders and geography as one nation linked to one territory. These assumptions had underpinned the belligerent displacement of Palestinians at the founding of Israel, the Israeli 'law of return', and the fantasy of an unbroken historical link to the land that justified Israel's excesses. Proposing to create a bi-national state meant no more than preserving this structure of ideas but in a more limited space.

Moreover, bi-nationalism permitted both communities to continue to believe they had a right to the whole land, and, since Israeli Jews were more advanced as a group, and better organised and wealthier than Palestinians, they would assert that feeling of ownership in social dominance over them. Nor would they ever cease to strive for the 'ingathering' of more Jews to the state to strengthen their community's position. Thus Uri Avnery's forecast of a disadvantaged Palestinian community of second-class citizens ending up in an unequal society was likely to come true. Though there existed no real parallel for the case of Israel/Palestine, the Cypriot example of attempted bi-nationalism between Greeks and Turks between 1960 and 1974 is instructive. There were Greek Cypriots who did not accept that Turks should have an equivalent status in the joint state, and who never gave up their view that Cyprus was Greek and a part of Greece, and so resented the Turkish presence. They showed this in vicious military assaults on the Turkish community and in numerous discriminatory ways. The whole experiment collapsed when Turkey, coming to the aid of its people, invaded Cyprus with consequences that are with us to this day.[85]

In a secular, democratic state, on the other hand, citizens would have rights not derived from membership of an ethnic or religious group. They would be equal before the law as individuals and not as groups, irrespective of race or religion. Such an arrangement would be useful in bypassing the difficulty of defining what in fact constituted the Israeli Jewish community. It was not homogenous, indeed how could it be, since it included people from places as culturally diverse as Morocco, Ethiopia and the US, as well as a good number of Jews from Russia? Thus the secular state would reflect more closely the multicultural reality on the ground and help create a society into which Palestinians would fit more naturally as part of a cultural mosaic. It would also conform more closely to a tradition long familiar to Arab and Islamic societies, that of pluralism, interaction and tolerance towards different ethnicities and faiths in their midst. This had been true, not only of the Islamic Empire at its zenith, but also in more recent times. Jews, fleeing persecution in Spain in the fifteenth century, found refuge and prospered in the lands of the Muslim Ottoman Empire, and in our own time religious minorities, even under the totalitarian regimes of Saddam

Hussein in Iraq and the Alawites in Syria, enjoyed equality with the rest. (It was only after the US/UK invasion of Iraq in 2003 and the resulting anarchy in the country that its Christian minority flocked to Syria for refuge and something more akin to the tolerance it had known before.[86]) Palestinian society in particular, before the mass immigration of European Jews imposed their exclusivist creed of Zionism and culturally alien philosophy on the country, had been a successful composite of Muslims, Christians and Jews, as well as Armenians, Circassians, Europeans and others.

In a secular state, religious practice and social customs are confined to the private sphere and do not inform state policy. Many Arabs feared that 'secular' meant 'atheist' and resisted this solution on that basis, but in fact it referred to nothing more than the separation of church and state, long familiar to Western liberal democracies such as Britain or the US. Unlike the bi-nationalist state, a secular democracy was likely to be conducive towards helping its citizens develop a common national identity through a sense of belonging to each other and to the state. Their loyalty to their shared state and sense of social cohesion would, in theory at least, be greater in such a situation because the state would not be competing with their own communities for that loyalty.[87] In this environment, the supremacist ideas, discrimination on ethnic or racial lines and sense of exclusive ownership of the whole land that we referred to above would be discouraged from continuing and begin to fade, even if very gradually. In time, the hope was that a new identity, developed as a result of this sharing, would permanently replace the previous ethnic or other divisive definitions.

Such aims would of course directly conflict with Zionism and spell its end, and so would not be acceptable to the majority of Jews. Though Tilley has called this view into question, arguing that Zionism did not strictly require an ethnic state with a Jewish majority, and under the right democratic conditions, could be compatible with the creation of a unitary state, this seems improbable, given the present evidence.[88] From the Palestinian point of view, however, the secular democratic solution was the better option. Only then could the country be returned to a semblance of what it had been before Zionism overtook it. Who knew, it could even turn out better as a result of the amalgam of enterprising Jews and Arabs cooperating to build a new society. Aside from those who latterly argued for a period of separation in their own state while they recuperated from the ordeal of Israeli occupation, and thus did not support a single state whatever its form, surely the only reason for Palestinians to choose bi-nationalism over secular democracy was because they believed that the other solution was impossible to attain. The three Palestinian respondents in my survey who supported the secular democratic state thought it was 'utopian', and the 22 respondents who were willing to share a state with Israelis qualified their answer with 'but only if they don't discriminate against us'.

Obstacles to the one-state solution

There is no doubt that as a solution, the one-state proposition posed an enormous challenge to entrenched positions and established ideas about how the conflict should be solved. The combination of the cultural/psychological dependence of Jews worldwide on the idea of Israel and the Western addiction to supporting this dependence were formidable obstacles. The end of the Jewish state inherent in the creation of a unitary Israel/Palestine was unthinkable in a context of long-standing Israeli denial of its true history: how it came into being, the resulting injustice done to the Palestinians and the indifference to their sufferings over most of the last century. That denial and the freedom from retribution allowed to Israel had

enabled several generations of Israeli Jews to enjoy the privileges of a settler colonialist enterprise without bearing the
costs. This and the anti-Arab racism that was an integral part
of keeping the Israeli project viable would be difficult to give
up. Discrimination in favour of Jews was structured into the
very fabric of the Jewish state and its institutions.

How would one persuade a people reared on such privileges and feelings of superiority to abandon them in return for
less prosperity and an uncertain future? And how could such
people, with a history of being minorities in every society
they had lived amongst and now found themselves a majority
for the first time, relinquish that status to become a part of
something once again? Equally problematic was the fact that,
when implanted into the Arab region, Israel never saw itself
as anything other than a Western state, and had no concept
of, or desire for, being a part of the Middle East, as would
have to happen if it merged with Palestine. Such a situation
would force on Israelis the unaccustomed prospect of revising
their instinctive fear of and contempt for Arabs. Hillel Frisch,
an Israeli academic I met at the Truman Institute in Jerusalem's Hebrew University in December 1999, told me without
a trace of embarrassment that Arab civilisation had nothing
to offer him or any other Jew. 'This so-called civilisation', he
said, 'stopped in the fourteenth century and so what's there to
learn from them now – democracy, technology, what?'

The one-state solution signified the end of Zionism as
a political ideology, but it allowed for the continuation of
'cultural Zionism', where Jews could maintain a Jewish cultural
identity in the biblical homeland. One Israeli Zionist who
seems to have accepted this distinction is the former speaker of
the Knesset, Avraham Burg, who wrote of his dismay at what
Israel had become: the 'perversions of the Israeli soul', as he
put it. Israelis could not assume that the existence of the state
was assured, and Burg saw the need to re-establish the con-

nection between Jews and 'the sources of Jewish culture' in an open, non-racist society that welcomed the Other.[89] However, so persuaded by political Zionism was the majority of Jews worldwide that they saw its demise as a sort of personal annihilation. It was an irony that in a situation where more than two-thirds of Jews do not live in Israel and apparently have no intention of doing so, they would still have fought for its survival. Such sentiments were difficult to dispel and posed another significant obstacle.

At the same time, the Western powers, which had lavished moral and material support on Israel since its inception, balked at the prospect of confronting the disaster they had created for a Middle East bogged down by an intractable conflict with no end in sight. Far from solving the Jewish question through creating the Jewish state, as they had hoped, the problem would return to face them if that state were dissolved. They were as anxious as any Zionist to resist a one-state outcome that would signal the defeat of the project they had espoused and expose the folly of their strategy over many decades. Their near-hysterical reaction to the Iranian President Mahmoud Ahmadinejad's provocative declaration in 2006 quoting the Ayatollah Khomeini that Israel should be 'wiped off the map', and the obsessive insistence that the Hamas government recognise Israel's 'right to exist' were indications of this sense of failure. The powerful Christian Zionists of America were no lesser champions of the Jewish state and, for their own fanatical reasons, would also fight any threat to its survival. Finally, it would take considerable effort to reverse the US's entrenched support for Israel, which had acquired the status of an adopted child for successive US governments. The US agenda for a Middle East with Israel at its heart would go up in smoke if Israel were subsumed in a unitary state, which reinforced the US's determination to ensure its survival.

No wonder then that, despite an impressive revival of the debate over its various aspects, which had entered mainstream political thinking, the unitary state was still far from being officially adopted as the preferred solution. Its proponents frequently looked to the example of South Africa, which had become a one-state democracy after the defeat of apartheid. In fact the cases were not as close as some commentators wanted to believe.[90] While many of apartheid's discriminatory practices were replicated in Israel's restrictions on Palestinian life, the two projects had basic differences. In South Africa, blacks were in the majority and the whites sought to rule over them, not to replace them. The struggle between the two communities was over rights, citizenship and equality, not, as in the Israeli/Palestinian case, over the possession of land. The defeat of apartheid came about after the withdrawal of foreign, especially US, support caused by a large-scale, external anti-apartheid campaign and, most importantly, economic sanctions, of which there was no sign in the Palestinian case.

There was no doubt that Israel and the apartheid South African regime had forged a close relationship over decades and were agreed on similar discriminatory measures in dealing with their 'subject' populations.[91] But raising the South African parallel, though usually dismissed by Israel and its supporters as antisemitic,[92] was useful to the Palestinian struggle, even if it did not exactly mirror their own situation, mainly because it helped to stimulate a debate about the concept of exclusivist states and the one-state solution.[93] It was also useful in emphasising by example the importance of repentance, the need for the former oppressor to admit and make amends for the wrongs inflicted on his victim. This was as indispensable for the Palestinians as it had been for South Africa. The South African Truth and Reconciliation Commission, established in 1995, after the defeat of apartheid, was set up to bear witness to and record the human rights violations perpetrated under the apartheid regime. It took testimony from thousands of abusers and their victims and allowed for a cathartic public exposé of previously unacknowledged crimes and unaddressed grievances. When it reported in 1998, the Commission set up a mechanism for victim reparation, including a compensation fund to which the beneficiaries of apartheid would be obliged to contribute.[94]

Although it might not have fulfilled all expectations or even been wholly successful – it was criticised for failing to achieve much reconciliation between the parties and for being weighted in favour of the abusers – the Truth and Reconciliation Commission nevertheless went to the heart of a psychological truth about human dealings. Conflicts rooted in injustice, as is the one in Palestine/Israel, need what the psychologists call 'closure', when the perpetrator acknowledges the injustice committed and makes visible and material reparation to the victim. It is only then that the conflict can definitively end and true reconciliation begin. From the start of their dispossession, it was a bitter bone of contention for Palestinians that Israelis had never so much as apologised for what they had done, let alone make amends for it. The insistence on the implementation of their right of return had also to be understood in this context: that for Israelis it would constitute the fairest and most definite act of repentance for crimes committed by Zionism, and in so doing they would have undone the state that it had created.

Can the one-state solution ever happen?

The foregoing account has shown how difficult it would be to implement the one-state solution. Yet that should not have been the starting point of the discussion. The question of whether this solution was *feasible* was frequently confused with whether it was *desirable*, and it was here that the struggle for hearts and minds should have started. Prolonged concentration on the two-state outcome as the only solution for the conflict had made it into a mantra that discouraged imaginative thinking. If one set aside the issue of feasibility, the advantages of the unitary state made it unarguably desirable. No other solution was able to satisfy the needs of justice for the Palestinians, including the refugees, and the needs of security for Israelis. Though these needs were frequently derided by Arabs who wondered why a state armed to the teeth and supported to the hilt by the world's one superpower should ever have felt insecure, Israeli Jewish fear was real.

Whatever its source – and most of my Palestinian survey respondents put it down to the fact that, as they said, thieves never rested easy while their victims were close by – Israeli insecurity is an important factor. Indeed, it was frequently invoked by Israel to justify its attacks on neighbouring states. My father, who had lost everything through the creation of Israel and yet who mainly blamed the British for allowing the tragedy to happen, viewed Jewish anxieties with empathy. He saw the whole Zionist project as nothing more than a product of this Jewish fear. Arabs did not understand that, he often said, and it was one reason for their inability to deal with Israel.

Making the one-state solution happen was going to be hard and its supporters looked to a far distant future for its fulfilment. 'Not in my lifetime,' many of them said, or 'it will take a hundred years or more', or 'my children may see it, but their children more like', and so on. Whatever the truth, this solution could not come about in a rush or by a miraculous conversion to the view that it was the only way forward. Nor could it be imposed by force of circumstance (as will be discussed later). It has to be seen as a slow process of evolving political and social awareness, campaigning and preparation, all of them entailing arduous struggle.[95] It could not be otherwise, given the monumental task of dismantling the structure and institutions of a state built on Zionism and replacing it with a genuinely democratic dispensation of equal rights and non-discrimination.

The leap for Israelis from a worldview of supremacy and exclusivism imposed by force to a humanist philosophy of peaceable coexistence and opposition to racism and violence would be a huge one. As would the leap for Arabs, from their position of rejection of any rights in Palestine for people they see as nothing more than colonisers, and enmity towards Israelis developed over decades, to an unqualified acceptance of them as equal partners. It also requires of Arabs the difficult task of re-defining their own national identity and a readiness to embrace a new and unique entity in the region, a Palestinian-Israeli state without precedent. The role of those Arab regimes that had based their *raison d'être* on hostility to Israel with all the military and economic developments that that entailed would need to be revised. As such, the consequences for the region would be profound.

It is not the purpose of this book to set out a blueprint for building the unitary state. One could write out a list of the traditional steps well known to all activists as to how one carries a political idea forward. This would include such things as political education, the creation of cadres and constituencies, enlisting the support of top politicians and decision-makers, and so on. But the main plank of the campaign was to start a debate amongst Palestinians and Jews about the one-state solution, to unify them around the concept, while at the same time ensuring that it became a part of the mainstream discourse. A two-state interim phase in which Palestinians replenished their shattered identities, regained normality and generally recovered from the Israeli occupation was a possible route to the end result, at least in theory (since the Palestinian state looked an unlikely eventuality, as discussed above). It was also a necessary aspiration to maintain in the short term so as not to create splits amongst the Palestinians. Too many of them had become attached to the idea of having their own state and too many still believed that the international community would help them achieve it, to throw away the chance. And indeed, in the unlikely event of its happening and with a policy of open borders, growing exchange and collaboration between the two states, that could have led to their eventual integration and, eventually, a one-state outcome. Likewise, a bi-national stage, reassuring Israelis and Palestinians that their national identities would not be subsumed in a single state before they were ready, was another possible route to the same end point.

An equal rights strategy

The foregoing has been a presentation of common-sense arguments for what is the only logical solution to this long-running conflict. But logic and common sense mean little in a situation of unequal power, where the stronger side has succeeded for over seventy years in imposing its will on the weaker side. Nor would persuasion, organisation and popular mobilisation, however promising they appeared, be sufficient to make it happen in time. And time is of the essence for the Palestinians, as their land is progressively eaten away by Israeli colonisation, their capital city, Jerusalem, increasingly judaised, and the return of refugees indefinitely delayed.

And yet, the way forward is at hand. By the start of 2022, the basic conditions for achieving a one-state solution in Israel/Palestine were in place. Not everyone recognised this fact, or wanted to, even though the reality on the ground was staring them in the face. Accustomed for decades to think in terms of the two-state solution, one that would deliver the longed-for state of their own, most Palestinians ignored anything that contradicted this vision. If they had not, they would have realised that from 1967 onwards Israel/Palestine had become a single state in all but name.

The real-life position was that the territory between the Jordan River and the Mediterranean Sea was one single entity, under the administration of one sovereign government, that of the state of Israel. The so-called Green Line, marking the 1949 armistice, that used to separate 1948-Israel from Jordanian-ruled East Jerusalem and the West Bank, and Egyptian-administered Gaza, had disappeared for all intents and purposes. Israel's resounding victory in the Arab–Israeli War of June 1967 enabled it to seize Palestinian (and Syrian) territory, which have been under military occupation to this day.

The result is that Israel/Palestine in 2022 was already one state, but it was an unequal one with differential rights and classes of citizenship. Its population comprised 6.6 million Israeli Jews with full citizenship and rights, 1.8 million Israeli Palestinians, also with citizenship but restricted rights, and 4.7 million Palestinians with no citizenship and no rights. This last group, as we saw above, was further handicapped by years of Israeli military rule, and myriad discriminatory practices. These were detailed in a damning 2017 UN report, quickly withdrawn from the UN's website following an outcry from Israel and the US,[96] that documented what it called the apartheid system imposed on the Palestinians by Israeli policy and its devastating effects. Two newer reports documented the same apartheid reality, the first by the Israeli human rights organisation, B'tselem, in January 2021,[97] and the second by Human Rights Watch in April 2021.[98] The latest on the same topic was Amnesty International's report, unequivocally titled 'Israel's apartheid against Palestinians: A cruel system of domination and a crime against humanity', released in February 2022.[99]

All of these were powerful critiques of Israel's discriminatory practices against the Palestinians under its rule.

Unsurprisingly, several World Bank reports, the latest in 2019, found that Israel's occupation of the West Bank had led to an 'unsustainable' economic situation, with zero growth and two out of three young people unemployed. Meanwhile, Israel's near-total blockade of Gaza's land, sea and airspace was causing chronic shortages of essential foods, medicines and construction materials. To punish Gazans for throwing incendiary devices over the barrier with Israel, Gaza's fishermen, on whom many depended for sustenance, were restricted in 2021 to a fishing limit of ten nautical miles, down from the twenty miles that were agreed under the Oslo Accord. A 2012 UN study had predicted that by 2020, Gaza's coastal aquifer would be damaged beyond repair, leaving its people without potable water, and the majority only kept alive by the support of external funding.

This man-made situation was the inevitable result of a long-standing Western policy of permissiveness towards Israel that allowed it to flout international law with impunity. How else could Israel have been left to rule over a population to which it had offered no citizenship or rights, while also denying them the protection of the Fourth Geneva Convention to which they were entitled as occupied people? Israel's pretext, that the 1967 Palestinian territories were 'disputed', not occupied, is not accepted in international law. But that did not deter Israel from behaving as a sovereign state in the occupied territories, considering itself free to act as it wished 'in its own land'.

Had it not been for the existence of the Palestinian Authority, set up by the Oslo Accords in 1996, this anomalous situation would have come to light decades ago. The illusion that the PA created in people's minds (the Palestinians included), of an independent government of a state-in-waiting, was extraordinarily effective in presenting the Israeli-Palestinian relationship as one of near equivalence. It obscured the

145

glaring inequality of occupier and occupied, and the reality of Palestinians as a people under colonial rule without legal rights. The internationally supported two-state solution which promised to create an independent Palestinian state, soon to join the community of nations, put the finishing touches to this false portrayal.

A smart PR campaign that accused Israel's critics of antisemitism was run to help Israel escape censure for its illegal system. This campaign was already working well in Europe and the US, where legislation against anti-Israel activities was being formalised in several countries. US backing for Israel had never been stronger, and as we saw, several Arab states reversed their previously hostile positions on Israel, and were making alliances with it.

It was for the Palestinians to draw the correct inference from the inequitable, one-state reality in which they lived. The American Jewish commentator (and former liberal Zionist), Peter Beinart, did just that in two remarkable articles. In the first, 'I no longer believe in a Jewish state' (*New York Times*, 8 July 2020), he recognised the one-state reality of Israel/Palestine and put forward a thesis of equal rights in that state. He described Israel as an unequal bi-national state, and recommended it become an equal state as the only way to gain stability. In a later article for *Jewish Currents* (27 April 2021), he went further and stated, 'There is no [Jewish] right to a state', an analysis of the right to self-determination used by Zionism to justify its seizure of Palestine. But that self-determination came at the cost of basic Palestinian rights.

Jewish self-determination violated Palestinian rights on a massive scale. It violated the rights of individual Palestinians living in the West Bank, East Jerusalem and the Gaza Strip by denying them citizenship in the country under whose rule they lived. It violated the individual rights even of those Palestinians who held Israeli citizenship by denying them equality under the law. And it violated the rights of Palestinian refugees and their descendants by preventing them from returning to the places from which they were expelled. For these reasons, Beinart concluded that the best solution is the creation of an 'equal state'.

For that to happen, Palestinians in their turn need to set aside the failed strategies of the past and examine the real options before them. Whatever long-term ambition they had nurtured for themselves, currently they lived unequal lives in a system that oppressed them. And that had to end. Only a demand for equal civil and political rights with the rest of the population ruled by Israel could address this immediate oppression and open a route to restoring their rights. At one stroke, an equal rights demand would put the ball in Israel's court: either it must vacate the Palestinian territories it occupied, or give their population equal rights with the rest – a straightforward, logical choice it would be interesting to see Israel refute.

There are some honourable antecedents to a Palestinian equal rights campaign. The South African freedom struggle aimed from the start for equality of rights of all citizens in a new democratic South Africa, and after 1948, for the overthrow of apartheid. Its message inspired an international anti-apartheid movement in 1960 that helped to end South Africa's system of discrimination against non-whites. For a time, it used armed struggle, but its tactics were mostly non-violent. A Palestinian Freedom Charter modelled on South Africa's was a good start. Though the parallels with the Palestine case are not exact, the struggles were alike enough for Nelson Mandela to say in a 1977 speech in Pretoria, 'We know too well that our freedom is incomplete without the freedom of the Palestinians.'

The civil rights movement of the mid-1950s in the southern United States makes another uplifting model for Palestinians to follow. Its origins in a long-standing American history of slavery are different, but its strategy to attain equal rights for

African Americans was an object lesson in peaceful, effective civil action for Palestinians to study. The movement's use of litigation, mass media publicity, boycotts, people's marches, sit-ins and civil disobedience inspired huge national support, that eventually forced the federal government to pass major civil rights legislation in 1964 and 1965.

The advantages for the Palestinians of an equal rights system are many: equal legal status, equal government representation – through which refugee repatriation could become policy, equal access to education, employment and social services, and the multiple benefits of a normal civic life that they never had under occupation. Above all, such a system would enable Palestinians to remain on their land. As Israeli journalist Gideon Levy pointed out in his article 'The single-state is already here' (*Haaretz*, 10 April 18), only a system of equal rights for everyone can make Israel a true democracy, with the prospect that it could be headed one day by a Palestinian president and a Jewish prime minister, or vice versa.

The obstacles in the way of implementing this idea are immense, and overlap with much that has already been mentioned. Zionists would see in it the end of Israel as a major-ity-Jewish state, and so the end of Zionism. Jewish Israeli citizens reared on a diet of supremacy and entitlement, and conditioned to hate and fear Arabs, would reject any attempt at equivalence with them. The Israeli state, accustomed to exploiting Palestine's land and resources, while subjugating its people, would not be prepared for an equal relationship with them.

The Palestinians for their part would regard an equal rights proposal as a defeat of the national project and the end of resistance to Israel. Whatever the rhetoric about equality, they would fear becoming second-class citizens, alongside the current Palestinian citizens of Israel. Those whose lives had been blighted by Israel's occupation wanted only to live in a separate state of their own. After the Oslo Accords, when hope of an independent state was running high, many Palestinians were encouraged to believe it would happen. I remember seeing dozens of foreign NGOs in Ramallah busily preparing the Palestinians for 'statehood'. They helped to entrench the idea to which many still cling.

Not least, all those who espoused the two-state solution would reject the idea as a negation of an internationally agreed position. Having secured United Nations backing for a Palestinian state on the 1967 territories as part of a two-state solution in several General Assembly resolutions, and recognition in 2012 of 'the State of Palestine' by a majority of 138 member states, they argued, why throw away those gains? Especially when, on the strength of it, Palestine was now accepted as a member of several international bodies like UNESCO and the International Criminal Court. In addition, opinion polls among Palestinians (and Israelis) had consistently shown support for two states, even though it fell to 43 per cent in 2018 (down from a high of 70 per cent in a 2013 Gallup poll). Lastly, the Palestinians' own formal representative, the PLO, was at the forefront of support for this solution, and would also oppose its overthrow.

No one could deny these were genuine objections. But by the same token, the reality on the ground was undeniable too. A glance at the map showed the logistical impossibility of a viable state in what remained of the 1967 territories, and a moment's reflection would underline the impossibility of trying to clear Israel's settlements out of them. Without a giant upheaval in the balance of world power, or a miraculous change of heart on the part of Western states, the two-state solution would remain out of reach. Unless some of those who espoused this solution could come up with an effective way of making it happen, continuing to push for it could be regarded as time-wasting and irresponsible.

Yet, as we have pointed out, the two-state solution, even if it did become reality, could not offer the Palestinians full justice. Only an equal rights system, grounded in equal respect for the needs of all citizens, could give the Palestinians the basic right to live decent lives in their own homeland, and eventually to repatriate those of their compatriots who were expelled in 1948 and thereafter. At the time of writing, there was no real constituency for this solution on either side, although the idea had started to attract interest amongst political thinkers and those who already supported a one-state solution. The PA's late senior negotiator, Saeb Erekat, was never one of those, but in 2017, after the US recognition of Jerusalem as Israel's capital, he announced the end of the two-state solution. 'Now is the time to transform the struggle for one state with equal rights for everyone,' he said.[100]

It will be difficult to accomplish, and can only be done in stages. The Palestinian Authority must first be persuaded to convert itself from a pseudo-government of a non-existent state with unrealistic aims into a campaigning body that leads the equal rights project. If that happened, a wide-ranging campaign would be instituted involving civic education, use of mass media to promote the idea internationally, recourse to international law, and networks of connection with like-minded individuals, organisations and states such as South Africa. This list is not exhaustive, but shows what might be done once the political decision over equal rights is made.

Supporters of Palestinian rights everywhere must swing behind this demand. Jewish Israelis who share this vision need to join the Palestinians in a joint struggle for equality. Creating a just society in place of Israel's current system that privileged one group over others is the only moral and realistic option for the future. It is also the best way to rectify the terrible wrong done by Zionism to Palestinians, and also to Jews.

CHAPTER SIX

Eleven Days In May

The dramatic events that took place in Israel-Palestine during May 2021 were a landmark in the history of the conflict.[1] For the first time, uprisings erupted simultaneously in all Palestinian communities under Israel's rule: East Jerusalem, the West Bank, Gaza, and the so-called 'mixed' Arab-Jewish towns and cities in 1948 Israel. Palestinians in refugee camps and in the diaspora worldwide came out in solidarity. It was a moment of unprecedented unity amongst all Palestinian groups, and engendered a strong feeling of optimism for a people long fragmented and without a collective future. As might be expected, the same events provoked Israel into lashing out in order to maintain the status quo. Its army and border police came down hard on all who defied its rule. As a result, 256 Palestinians, including 66 children, and 13 Israelis were killed, 1,900 Gazans were injured, and 72,000 of Gaza's people were made homeless.

The sequence of events was rapid and developed over eleven days: 6–21 May. The uprisings started in Jerusalem in two hotspots: the Al-Aqsa Mosque, and Sheikh Jarrah, a neighbourhood of East Jerusalem. A little-reported incident at the mosque on 13 April, the beginning of the Muslim holy month of Ramadan, prepared the ground for what happened later. Israeli police severed the loudspeaker cables of the minaret from which the call to prayer sounds out, in order that Israel's president could make an address from the nearby Western Wall undisturbed. Soon afterwards, police put up barriers at the Damascus Gate into the Old City, preventing Palestinians from congregating at a favourite meeting place for them after prayer at the mosque. Furious protests followed.

Into this charged atmosphere, Lehava, an extremist Israeli right-wing group, started marching through East Jerusalem, chanting, 'Death to Arabs', and attacking Palestinian homes. Tensions rose rapidly, and the police attacks on the Aqsa mosque increased. On 8 May, *Laylat-u'l Qadr*, the most sacred night of Ramadan, Israeli troops stormed the mosque compound, injuring 600 people. The spectacle of tear gas canisters and stun grenades being lobbed into the mosque itself while worshippers were at prayer drew protests from world leaders. On 10 May, Hamas in Gaza served Israel an ultimatum for its assault on the Al-Aqsa mosque: to withdraw from the mosque and from Sheikh Jarrah (see below) by 6 p.m., or face the consequences. Israel ignored the ultimatum.

While all this was happening in the Old City, protests were being held in nearby Sheikh Jarrah over threatened house evictions. Sheikh Jarrah was a well-known Jerusalem neighbourhood, which had been home to many prominent Jerusalem Palestinians, and foreign diplomatic missions. In 1956, the Jordanian government, which then ruled Jerusalem and the West Bank, built houses for 28 families displaced from parts of Palestine that had been incorporated into the Israeli state in 1948. These became their homes in which their children were born and raised.

In 1972, two Jewish settler groups claimed that the land where the houses stood was legally theirs, and demanded the families pay them rent if they wanted to stay on. Even then, three of the families were evicted between 2003 and 2009, and six more were facing the same fate. Israel's Supreme Court had been due to pronounce in May on the outcome of the families' court case against their evictions, but was forced to postpone its decision because of the protests. Few people believed, on past evidence of Israeli justice, that when the court re-convened the families' case would succeed.

From 6 May onwards, Palestinians in solidarity with the families held nightly vigils in Sheikh Jarrah, to which Israel's police responded by shutting off all access to the area, throwing tear gas and shock grenades at protestors, and shooting rubber bullets. Skunk water was sprayed inside the houses, restaurants and cafes, which made the residents' lives intolerable. Belligerent Jewish settlers, allowed in by the police, added harassment to this list of assaults.

Unrest had meanwhile spread to towns in Israel with large Arab communities. These rose up in protest first in Lod (Lydda), where on 11 May, the mayor was panicked into calling for border police reinforcements, curfews were imposed, and a state of emergency was declared. Synagogues, Jewish homes and Jewish-owned cars were set on fire, and there was widespread looting of Jewish homes. Police arrested over a thousand people, 159 of whom were Jews; and on 24 May, a further 1,555 arrests were made, almost all Arab.

On 12 May, protests spread to Ramla and Acre, and on 13 May to Beersheba, Tiberias, Haifa and Jaffa, where rioting, stabbing, shooting, arson and attempted house invasions were reported. Border police, notorious for their cruelty and ill treatment of Arabs, were deployed everywhere. Aggressive settlers were shunted into the places of protest to threaten and intimidate the Arab population. Of all the places of unrest, the riots in Israel's towns and villages were extremely alarming to the government. The Arabs here were traditionally docile and not given to protest, with some exceptions. For them to rise up in this way caused Israel's Defence Minister Benny Gantz to declare it was 'no less dangerous than Hamas rockets', and Israel's president warned of an impending civil war.[2]

On the West Bank protests erupted on 14 May in Hebron, Ramallah, Nablus, Bethlehem, and an additional two hundred

One State

locations. Daily demonstrations took place, and the Israeli Army killed an estimated twenty people. These protest were the more remarkable for happening in a territory that Israel had criss-crossed with checkpoints and barriers in order to restrict movement between towns and villages. The PA's security forces further restricted people's freedom of protest and assembly. Yet, such was the strength of solidarity with events in Jerusalem and Gaza, that protestors still managed to defy the restrictions and come out in large numbers.

On 18 May, a general strike was called in all Palestinian areas on both sides of the old Green Line in protest against Israel's occupation and bombardment of Gaza. Shops in the West Bank, Gaza, and the towns and villages in 1948 Israel all shut down, and educational establishments closed. Economic activity was suspended throughout those areas, an expression of unified resistance not seen since the General Strike of 1936. It was a striking show of collective action and solidarity.

The final arena in which this cataclysm of resistance played out was Gaza. Hamas, having delivered its ultimatum on 10 May and finding it ignored by Israel, commenced firing rockets at Israeli towns.[3] Innovations to these rockets, developed since the last Gaza war, improved their military performance considerably. This time, they were fired daily in salvos of 50, rather than one by one as in the past. This made them more terrifying to people and more difficult to intercept. Some were able to reach Tel Aviv, Jerusalem, Beersheba, and even Eilat, 155 miles away. These are record distances and a clear advance on the weapons of 2014. Ashdod and Ashkelon, nearer targets, were hit repeatedly. Rocket barrages of 300 to 450 continued daily, undeterred by Israel's massive bombardment of Gaza. Israel's airports had to be shut down, and the inhabitants of targeted Israeli cities moved in panic to bomb shelters.

Hamas's arsenal included drones, drone submarines, mortars and anti-tank weapons of varying efficacy. Israel's missiles, drones and Iron Dome were largely able to protect its population from these weapons, but not completely. The Israeli Defence Forces claimed that 90 per cent of rockets were intercepted, but this turned out to refer to rockets capable of causing damage, with the rest getting through. A total of 4,300 rockets were fired in those eleven days, nearly all of them manufactured in workshops in Gaza. That meant more would be made to replace what was lost, and those were likely to be more advanced than the present ones.

In retaliation (and for once, the roles were reversed, Hamas having started the attack), Israel launched a massive campaign of bombing by air and sea.[4] There were 1,500 strikes daily, using F-16s, F-35s fitted with precision guided bombs and other state-of-the-art weaponry, and inflicted enormous damage on Gaza. By 16 May, four huge high-rise buildings in Gaza City, containing a complex of residential apartments, businesses, and offices, had been demolished; one of them, bombed on 15 May, housed the offices of Aljazeera and the Associated Press. Government buildings, five banks (on the basis they held Hamas accounts), and many residences, especially those where Hamas leaders lived, were demolished. Using bunker busters, Israel claimed it had destroyed about 25 per cent of the Hamas tunnel infrastructure where weapons were smuggled in and stored. Hamas refuted this, saying it had lost only 5 per cent of the tunnel networks.

Israel also claimed it had destroyed 340 Hamas rocket launchers and military boats, and killed 225 Hamas and 25 Islamic Jihad fighters. These figures were denied, Hamas saying it had lost 57 men, and Islamic Jihad, 21. In addition, 53 schools, 6 hospitals and 11 health centres, including Gaza's Covid vaccination centre, were destroyed; Gaza's largest bookshop and its desalination plant were demolished. The

Beach refugee camp was attacked, and the head of Gaza's vaccine programme, in addition to one of only two neurologists in Gaza, were killed. Most serious of all was the damage done to Gaza's infrastructure. Israel bombed main roads, water and sewage pipes and electricity cables, with the result that, according to Gaza sources, 800,000 people were without drinking water, and down to five hours of electricity a day.

In eleven days, Israel had mounted an assault on Gaza so devastating as to put Hamas out of action for years to come, or so Israel hoped. The deliberate targeting of Gaza's infrastructure was designed to cripple the population and their leaders. On 18 May, France, Egypt and Jordan filed for a UN Security Council resolution to approve a ceasefire, and on 21 May, a ceasefire, brokered by Egypt, Qatar and the UN, came into effect.

These events had marked effects on public opinion in the West. The surge in global Palestinian solidarity, most significantly in the US, was unmistakable. Twenty-four Democratic members of Congress came out in open support of the Palestinians, among them the vocal trio of Rashida Tlaib, Ilhan Omar and Alexandria Ocasio-Cortez, all of whom already held a strongly pro-Palestinian position. This created a feeling of threat amongst pro-Israel Republicans, as a result of which a group went out to Israel at the end of May to affirm their commitment to Israel's 'right to defend itself' against Hamas.

At the same time, social media, used predominantly by younger generations, became more strongly pro-Palestinian. Facebook was attacked for censoring anti-Israel posts, and students at many US campuses increased their pro-Palestinian solidarity. The Black Lives Matter (BLM) movement declared its identification with the Palestinian struggle for equality.[5] At their demonstration in New York on 31 May to mark the anniversary of George Floyd's death, this was vividly encapsulated in a placard which read, 'We can't breathe since 1948.'[6] The Palestinians in their turn affirmed their solidarity with BLM.

President Biden's administration found itself unprepared for this situation. It would have been natural and comfortable for Biden to follow a succession of supportive Israel-right-or-wrong US administrations, and that is what would have happened but for the May events. Biden did not have an Israel-Palestine policy to face these events beyond the traditional support for Israel that saw the US veto statements on the situation at the UN, reject UN calls for a ceasefire, make public affirmations of support for Israel's security concerns, and continue to supply arms to Israel. When the violence in Gaza was at its height, Biden approved an emergency payment of $735 million to compensate Israel for its losses of Iron Dome batteries and other armaments used to bomb Gaza.[7] Even so, he privately urged Israel's prime minister to accept a ceasefire, sent out his envoy Antony Blinken to Israel and the Palestinian Authority sooner than he might otherwise have done, and declared his commitment to the two-state solution.

Meanwhile, enthusiasm for the cause of Palestine surged in Europe. A London pro-Palestinian demonstration on 22 May attracted over 180,000 people, the largest ever such demonstration, and was accompanied by solidarity demonstrations in many British cities. Similar demonstrations took place in France and other European countries. Suddenly, the Palestine cause was back in the public eye more strongly than ever, in spite of Israel's best efforts for many decades to bury it.

The effect of the May uprisings on the Palestinians themselves was no less striking. While those injured by Israel's military assaults excited the sympathy of all Palestinians, there was also an exhilaration, a feeling that something was changing. The tragic routine of Israeli brutality, Palestinian defiance without result, and international indifference, was being challenged at last. This time, it looked to many Palestinians as if something new was happening. Hamas rockets, far from arousing criticism, were seen as the resistance of an unbowed people, who, despite the heavy cost of that resistance, refused to be cowed into passivity by Israel and its backers. The unity of resistance everywhere there was a Palestinian community was unprecedented, and all felt as one.

Noticeably, the Western media started to present the Palestinian story with a measure of fairness not seen before. The *New York Times*' front page of 26 May reproduced a series of emotive pictures of the children killed in Gaza under the moving title, 'They were only children'. Though the accompanying text pointed to Hamas as the perpetrator, the image was so powerful that it had a huge impact. The former head of the Anti-Defamation League in the US was provoked into cancelling his subscription to the paper in disgust. Peter Beinart's articles, highly critical of Israel, were appearing in the paper regularly, and later, several outspoken pieces by Palestinians appeared as well.[8] This tendency was replicated in Britain, and elsewhere.

The May 2021 uprisings were a cause for great optimism amongst Palestinians. Had Palestine's struggle reached a turning point, people wondered? Would the fightback against Israel, begun so promisingly, advance and progress until a resolution was reached? Israel had been rattled by the unity of Palestinian resistance, and had responded with characteristic force and repression. A ceasefire agreed between the parties to end the fighting was breached just hours after it took place; Aljazeera reported that Israeli police had fired tear gas on worshippers at the Al-Aqsa Mosque compound after Friday prayers on 21 May. But how long could Israel dam the tide of an invigorated Palestinian resistance?

As it turned out, Israel did just that – for the time being at least. Once again it showed it was able to confound public opinion and evade censure for its blatant abuses. Things quietened down, and there was a return to business as usual between Israeli occupier and Palestinian occupied: more assaults on Gaza; more arbitrary arrests, imprisonments, and killings of Palestinians in the West Bank. According to the Palestinian Ministry of Health, the number of Palestinian dead across the West Bank since the beginning of 2022 was 98, the highest for seven years; a further 51 were killed in Israeli attacks on Gaza in August 2022.[9]

In reality, however, things *had* changed. Flashpoints soon appeared, centred on the major West Bank cities, most especially Jenin and Nablus, and spreading to the areas around Ramallah.[10] Palestinian fighters, two of them from Jenin, killed 19 Israelis in a wave of attacks inside Israel from March to May 2022. In Nablus, where the PA seemed to have lost control of the situation, armed fighters from Hamas, Islamic Jihad, Fateh and the PFLP engaged Israeli forces in almost daily clashes.[11] In an effort to quash the unrest, the Israeli Army started to launch daily raids on Jenin and Nablus. In August, Israel carried out what it explained was a 'pre-emptive' attack on Islamic Jihad in Gaza.

Reports began to appear of the emergence of a new, more organised Palestinian armed resistance in the West Bank to complement the long-standing one in Gaza. This comprised the so-called 'Jenin and Tubas Brigades', and a generation of young fighters in Nablus extending to the villages outside Ramallah. They had in common their rejection of both Israel and the PA, which was seen as being in collusion with Israel, and they were prepared to shoot at military checkpoints and in clashes with the army. However, such activities were mainly defensive in nature, aiming to protect local areas from Israeli attack. To have engaged in aggressive action would require operating in larger areas and would need more advanced organisation than was available at the time.

Even so, these young fighters were beginning to have an impact both on the PA and on Israel. Whether and how this situation would develop in future was unknown; but Israel could be relied on to continue its violent crackdowns, provoking further Palestinian resistance. For example, in early October 2022, at the time of writing, Israel imposed a blockade on the Shu'fat refugee camp in East Jerusalem in response to the killing of an Israeli soldier at the checkpoint outside. Over 100,000 camp inhabitants were cut off inside while essentials ran out, prompting UNRWA to declare the situation 'unacceptable'.[12] Widespread Palestinian protests erupted throughout East Jerusalem in response.[13]

It was not likely these cycles would stop while the cause that first brought them into existence remained.

Conclusion: The Future

This book has explored the various parameters of the Israel–Palestine problem and why, despite the many proposals put forward for its resolution, it has remained insoluble. It was shown that the major reason for this failure was that one of the parties to the conflict, Israel, was allowed to impose its own vision for the future, which meant colonising Palestinian land and excluding or expelling its inhabitants, largely unencumbered by outside pressure or interference. It was this laissez-faire attitude on the part of the international community, and especially the US, that led ultimately to the current impasse.

What future can be envisaged for this conflict? There are today only these problematic outcomes possible: a) to allow the present situation to continue, b) to partition the land into an Israeli state and a collection of Palestinian enclaves named a Palestinian state, and c) to share the land in one unitary state.

Of this list, only the third option, as argued in Chapter 5, stood any chance of enduring in the long term. That is because it was the only just arrangement to resolve a conflict whose essence was injustice. It had become customary never to address the root causes of the conflict – Palestinian dispossession and its consequences. That position led to a series of peace proposals, each of them flawed by inequality between the two sides, and the deliberate omission of the refugee issue from any solution. For these reasons, they would not have endured, even had they been implemented.

To summarise, the most persistent of these 'non-solutions' was the proposal that took shape after 1974 to partition the old Mandate Palestine into two states, one, Israeli, on four-fifths of the land and the other, Palestinian, on the remaining fifth. As we saw, this inequitable solution continued to be put forward, despite the reality on the ground of a decimated portion allotted to the Palestinians, the near-annexation to Israel of almost half the West Bank territory, the barrier wall which was relentlessly drawing a new border between the two sides in Israel's favour and nothing like the 1967 lines meant to delineate a Palestinian state, as well as the total isolation of Gaza, and the loss of East Jerusalem to Israel, as its capital city. Most important of all was the geo-political reality of what had become in effect one state between the Mediterranean Sea and the Jordan River, ruled by one sovereign Israeli government.

Crucially, the favoured two-state solution never provided any countercheck on the power imbalance between the two sides, an imbalance so huge as to ensure that the stronger party, Israel, could always determine events in its favour. It also put Israel under no obligation to accept any proposal with which it disagreed. This unaccountability was vividly illustrated by the total impunity with which the Israeli Army repeatedly attacked the Palestinian territories, and at times, Syria and Lebanon.

It was beyond belief that in 2022 the people of Gaza could have been subjected for 15 years to the inhumane conditions of a deadly siege without any effective attempt on the part of the world community to end it. Such gross Israeli abuses of power have led me to wonder more than once why it was that Israel did not go the whole way: bomb Gaza to smithereens, for example, deport the Palestinians en masse, and raze their towns and villages to the ground. Who would have stopped Israel had it done so? Certainly not the European powers, which meekly followed the US's lead, and not the Arab states, which were incapable of independent action. And of all the Muslim states which supported the Palestine cause, only Iran espoused it fully, but whether it would ever be in a position to challenge the US-Israeli axis on Palestine's behalf was unknown and unlikely.

Not once in the last 75 years had Israel failed to accomplish what it wanted, if not immediately then later, as its steady progression from fledgling state to regional superpower convincingly shows. That success was like an intoxicating drug for Israelis, making them impervious to the need for their leaders to seek peaceful relations with their neighbours. So long as Israel was powerful enough to smite the Arabs if they showed the slightest opposition, Israel had no interest in a deal except on its own mean terms. We saw how the other side shifted considerably to accommodate the Israeli position, as the Oslo Accords and other Arab peace proposals showed. For Israel, however, that was not enough and it continued to take more and offer less.

While that remains the case, it is evident that the two-state solution cannot succeed, and, so long as Israel remains a Zionist state enjoying unabated Western support *as such*, things will never be any different. The Jewish state must, by its very nature, fight on to maintain itself as ethnically separate, supremacist and privileged. Any retraction from this position, however small, would open a Pandora's box of unpalatable questions that Israel and its creators do not want to answer. Why, for example, should such an anomalous state, out of step with the regional culture, language, religion and *Weltanschauung*, ever have been established in the Middle East? It should have seemed inevitable that people mostly accustomed to seeing humanity as divided into Jews and eternally hostile Gentiles, whom they had constantly to protect themselves against, could never have blended into the region or made for good neighbours.[1] More importantly, most Israelis held the Arabs and particularly the Palestinians in contempt. This was a theme running through Zionist history from the start. Such people would fight every attempt to integrate them – the *sine qua non* of any proper solution – would reject it as an attempt to 'Arabise' them, and would maintain their special bond with the Jews outside the region and with the West. Only through such links could they maintain their sense of themselves as the centre of world Jewry and a part of Western civilisation.

The future

That a state with such an ethnically biased, exclusivist ideology as Israel's can survive in this rigid form indefinitely must be open to question. But the logic of allowing it to remain in its present hegemonic form meant that there could be no long-term peaceful settlement, and the short-term future would be one of recurrent strife. In these conditions, a settlement in the form of Ariel Sharon's Jordanian option would have made sense from Israel's point of view, and represented for the West a last effort to salvage the two-state solution from the wreckage of Israel's leavings in the West Bank; hence the variations on this theme that included Donald Trump's Middle East plan of 2020.[2] But many practical and political problems stood in the way of this option, as already explained, which made it an unlikely outcome.

Of the future options listed above, the one most likely to prevail was the first, that of maintaining the status quo. So long as Israel remained powerful and had the backing of Western states, it was unrealistic to hope for any other, least of all the one-state alternative for which we laid out several cogent strategies. In a different world, one of those principled, peaceable plans would have succeeded But in the case of Israel-Palestine, the attainment of one, democratic, state was fated to come about in a very different way.

By 2021, the signs of widespread Palestinian frustration and resistance, which had been in evidence in the First Intifada, had only grown with time. How else could one interpret

Hamas's dogged persistence in developing its rocket capability, remarkable for a movement forced to operate under constant Israeli attack, and from 2007 under siege? Israel managed to conceal this heroic reality by treating Hamas and, by implication, everyone in Gaza as 'terrorists' that it needed to defend its citizens against, however ruthlessly. This lie was tacitly accepted by Israel's Western backers, and it was left to the UN and aid agencies to pick up the pieces after each Israeli war on Gaza.

A prophetic Israeli writer described the situation 15 years ago as 'explosive, unstable and impractical', that carried within it 'the beginnings of an intifada of resistance which will be more violent than those before and which will put before Israel choices that threaten its very existence'.[3] He could have been writing about the uprisings of May 2021. Was that to be the moment when everything changed? Many Palestinians thought so at the time, although similar dramas had happened before, only to quieten down and return to 'normal' – and every time they did, Israel went on to commit even more abuses of Palestinian rights, while still enjoying Western favour.

But what if that pattern was not repeated this time, and Palestinians had found a taste of unity and common struggle with each other that impelled them to refuse a return to the status quo ante – especially given the uprisings of Palestinians in 1948-Israel who had joined the fight? These were important partners in the struggle, albeit dangerous for Israel: resistance inside the heart of the state would be difficult to defeat if it persisted.

What if the uprisings we saw in May 2021 recurred with greater frequency and force? As we observed, indications that this might already be happening were in evidence in 2022, a year after the May uprisings, and could be expected to increase, especially as many Palestinians finally began to understand they were on their own in the struggle against Israel. No country or army, and certainly not the PA's militia, had come to their rescue, in spite of Israel's repeated and illegal assaults on them. And so they would have to go it alone, building new groups and working together against the enemy.

In such a scenario, what would Israel do? On past performance, we can anticipate a knee-jerk response to defend Zionism and safeguard the state with overwhelming force. Israel would intensify its anti-Palestinian repression, accelerate its colonisation programme, go on building the wall, and try to expel or starve out the Palestinians to thin their numbers. At the same time, the worldwide army of Israel's supporters would be mobilised to stifle the faintest anti-Israel criticism, and silence Palestinian voices everywhere it mattered. Antisemitism allegations would feature largely in this campaign, and attempts at influencing government legislation in Western states to outlaw criticism of Israel and Zionism would be intensified. These methods had already been shown to succeed in the West, and would be intensified for that reason.[4]

As a result of these attacks, Palestinians would feel they had no choice but to continue resisting by every means, and this time, they might carry world public opinion with them, which at the time of writing had shifted in their favour more than at any time previously. If nothing else, the recurring rounds of fighting showed that Hamas could not be eradicated as an opposition force and would need to be reckoned with each time Israel went on the attack. Connections between these fighters and the resistance movements in other areas of Palestine-Israel, which already existed, would be strengthened. With local leaderships, coordination and resources, uprisings would eventually be effective in countering and in time defeating Israel.

Conclusion: The Future

But even if that level of organisation did not exist, sooner or later, the Palestinian territories would rise up again, and over time would become more radicalised and ungovernable, something that had previously been difficult to envisage, given the PA's restrictive control of the West Bank. But there is nothing to say that control would persist, given the PA's unpopularity, and its ageing, widely discredited president, Mahmoud Abbas. A new generation of fighters in the West Bank emerged in 2021 who openly rejected the PA, and adopted armed resistance in direct opposition to the PA's peaceful strategy. These young fighters were not likely to disappear, and the cycle of Israeli savagery and military violence, followed by Palestinian retaliation, would repeat itself more frequently.

Eventually, and after much chaos and bloodshed, the barriers erected by Israel would disintegrate and a bi-national situation, if not a state, would come about, not in an orderly manner but willy-nilly. The entry of Palestinians into what Israelis had always wanted to be an exclusive club for Jews might prompt those who had the means to leave the country. These would most likely be the Jews of European origin who always saw themselves as part of the Western world anyway, and those for whom life with Arabs was unpalatable (often the same people). Emigration from the Jewish state at times of crisis had often been a well-kept secret of Israeli life. During the short-lived conflict with Lebanon in July 2006, for example, the rate of emigration from Israel increased five-fold, and the US and Canadian consulates were flooded with visa applications.[5] As the Israeli writer Irit Linur lamented many years ago in *Haaretz* (24 September 2004):

Life in Israel is of a trial period, and anyone who can get his hands on more glittering options abroad should take advantage of them … We, the aware and the correct, all too often see the State of Israel the way it is seen in Europe: a country on probation, a home on probation.

Today, that is still the case.

The remaining Israeli population would be composed of the poor, the ultra-religious, the *mizrahi* Jews and many of those born in the state who felt they belonged nowhere else. So a new situation would develop: a state for Jews and Palestinians, not through a managed process of orderly transition, but through chaos, displacement, the creation of new refugees and the deaths of many people on both sides. And in the end, all that the Zionist experiment would have accomplished would be to have postponed the inevitable for a few decades.

The Middle East has absorbed myriad communities, no matter what their origins, and the hotchpotch of European and oriental Jewish migrants and their descendants who had formed the Israeli community would be no exception. In time, they too would become part of the region, as if the state of Israel had never been. The pity of it was that it should have taken so much destruction, death and suffering to return history to its initial point of departure.

The fact is, of course, that the Zionist project was flawed from the start and Israel should never have been set up. The best solution to this intractable problem ideally would be to turn back the clock before there was any Jewish state and rerun history from there. I recall making this point at a meeting in London in 1978, one of the first of its kind between a few of us Palestinians and a handful of Israelis who defined themselves as anti-Zionist or non-Zionist. Their shock and surprise at such sentiments were evident, and all of them rejected my comment as a personal attack on them. What made them think, I remember wondering, that Palestinians could ever have wanted a foreign settler community to set up a state in their country?

It was perverse for Zionists to believe that the Palestinians could ever have vanished or become irrelevant. As Meron Benvenisti put it:

> The Zionist dream was maimed from the outset. It didn't take into account the presence here of another national group. Therefore, from the moment the Zionist movement decided that it was not going to exterminate the Arabs, its dream became unattainable.[6]

But Benvenisti did not see that even had Israel eradicated the Palestinian population, there was still the wider Arab world to contend with, hugging its every border. 'If Israel remains a colonialist state in its character, it will not survive,' wrote Haim Hanegbi. 'In the end the region will be stronger than Israel, in the end the indigenous people will be stronger than Israel.'[7] Zionism's ethos was not about peaceful coexistence but about colonialism and an exclusivist ideology to be imposed and maintained by force.

All the same, the clock will not go back and, although the Jewish state cannot be uncreated, it might be, so to speak, unmade. The reunification of Palestine's shattered remains in a unitary state for all its inhabitants, old and new, is the only realistic, humane and durable route out of the morass. It is also the only way for the Israeli Jewish community (as opposed to the Israeli state) to survive in the Middle East. To quote Haim Hanegbi once more, 'Anyone who wants to ensure the existence of a Jewish community in this country has to free himself from the Zionist pattern ... Because as things are now, there is no chance. A Jewish nation-state will not take hold here.'[8]

The inevitable end point

The scenario outlined above is not based on wishful thinking. Nor can one discount Israel's considerable ability to fight back and dominate from a position of global power and influence. Nevertheless, the situation in Palestine-Israel was inherently unstable and could not hold in its current form for long. In a way, it was too late for Israel to keep using the old thinking and the old methods. The Palestinians and their cause were too entrenched in the global public consciousness to be dismissed in 2022.

Even if the next uprising takes a different form, it cannot be averted. And what emerges at the end has been the main concern of this book. Our review of the tremendous obstacles facing the one democratic state solution may be daunting to some of those who support it in theory. But the fact that something is difficult to realise does not make it any less the right thing to do. Nor does the attainment of the one democratic state hinge solely on the wishes of Israel and its supporters. Other factors, though now unforeseen or thought improbable, could intervene and alter the situation dramatically: for example, a change in US foreign policy or a renaissance of Arab power, or some other extraordinary circumstance. Any of these could make a radical difference to Palestinian fortunes, although none of them has yet happened and some might never do so.

If and when they do, such events will merely dictate the pace and timing of the one democratic state solution. But the concept itself must have been established long before, not as an immediately attainable goal perhaps, but as a vision, an aspiration and a belief in the ultimate humanity of Palestinians and Jews and all those who wish to see them prosper.

Notes

Introduction

1. Shlomo Sand, *The Invention of the Jewish People* (London: Verso, 2009).
2. Benjamin Haddad, 'How Europe became pro-Israel', *Foreign Policy*, 20 May 2021.
3. Rex Brynen, 'Palestinians and the Arab state system: Permeability, state consolidation, and the Intifada', *Canadian Journal of Political Science*, Vol. 24, No. 3 (1991), pp. 552–621.
4. Sanya Mansoor, 'How online activism and the racial reckoning in the US have helped drive a groundswell of support for Palestinians', *Time*, 21 May 2021.

1   The Problem of Zionism

1. Ari Shavit, 'Survival of the fittest'. *Haaretz*, 8 January 2004.
2. Z. Jabotinsky, *Writings: On the Road to Jerusalem*, cited in A. Shlaim, *The Iron Wall: Israel and the Arab World* (London: Allen Lane, 2000), pp. 13–14. See also Lenni Brenner, *The Iron Wall: Zionist Revisionism from Jabotinsky to Shamir* (London: Zed Books, 1984), pp. 73–5.
3. Moshe Dayan, *Milestones: An Autobiography* [Hebrew], (Jerusalem: Edanim Publishers, 1976), cited in Shlaim, *The Iron Wall*, p. 101.
4. D. Ingrams, *Palestine Papers, 1917–1922: Seeds of Conflict* (London: John Murray, 1972), p. 73.
5. The Balfour Declaration, named after Britain's Foreign and Colonial secretary of the time, Lord Arthur Balfour, was issued in 1917, It was addressed to the Britsh Zionist leadership, and offered to facilitate the creation of a 'national home for the Jewish people' in Palestine, at a time when Britain had no

control of the country it was offering. Nevertheless, the Zionists seized upon it to legitimise their claim to Palestine.

6. Akiva Orr, *The Un-Jewish State: The Politics of Jewish Identity in Israel* (London: Ithaca Press, 1983), pp. 228–9.

7. '218 Indians officially converted in India', *Ynetnews*, 5 October 2006.

8. Israel Ministry of Foreign Affairs, 'Jewish Agency plans fast-track conversions for immigrants from CIS', 7 March 2003.

2   Israel and the Arabs

1. Ella Shohat, *On the Arab-Jew, Palestine, and Other Displacements* (London: Pluto Press, 2017), pp. 77–83.

2. United Nations Development Programme, *The Arab Human Development Report, 2002–03*; N. Fergany interview in *Al-Ahram Weekly*, 14 July 2002.

3. Hogr Tarkhani, 'Strengthening relations between Israel and Iraqi Kurdistan', *Jerusalem Post*, 12 June 2022.

4. 'Southern Sudan's president hails bilateral relations with Israel', *Sudan Tribune*, 15 June 2022.

5. Meir Yoav Stern, *Maariv*, 31 October 2005.

6. Since 2004 Turkey has objected to Israeli secret agents operating in the Kurdish areas of Northern Iraq; see Seymour Hersh, 'Plan B', *The New Yorker*, 28 June 2004.

7. J. Abadi and J. Krischer, 'Israel and the Horn of Africa – the strategic and political imperatives', *Journal of South Asian and Middle Easter Studies*, Vol. 25 (2002), pp. 41–64.

8. B. Milton-Edwards, *Islamic Politics in Palestine* (London: I.B. Tauris, 1996), pp. 103–44.

9. Robert Dreyfuss's *Devils' Game: How the United States Helped Unleash Fundamentalist Islam* (New York: Henry Holt, American Empire Project Series, 2005), is highly illuminating on the Israel-Hamas relationship.

10. S. Kedourie and S.G. Haim, 'Introduction: Writers on Arab nationalism', in *idem* (eds), *Arab Nationalism: An Anthology* (Berkeley: University of California Press, 1976), pp. 3–72.

Notes

11. Benny Morris, *The Birth of the Palestinian Refugee Problem Revisited* (Cambridge: Cambridge University Press, 2004); Ilan Pappe, *The Making of the Refugee Problem 1947–51* (London: I.B. Tauris, 1992).

12. J. Dash, 'Doing good in Palestine: Magnes and Henrietta Szold' in W.M. Brinner and M. Rischin (eds), *Like All the Nations? The Life and Legacy of Judah L. Magnes* (New York: State University of New York Press, 1987), pp. 99–111.

13. Y. Porath, *In Search of Arab Unity, 1930–1945* (London: Frank Cass, 1986), pp. 600–601.

14. Ben-Gurion never accepted the part relating to the creation of a Palestinian state. See Simha Flapan, *The Birth of Israel: Myths and Realities* (New York: Pantheon Books, 1987), p. 37.

15. David Ben-Gurion in *Letters to Paula*, cited in Shlaim, *The Iron Wall*, p. 21.

16. Exact figures for the totality of the world Palestinian population are hard to obtain. Statistics in use are based on a mixture of UN refugee numbers and estimates for the rest. The Palestinian Central Bureau of Statistics estimated a world Palestinian population of 10.1 million at the end of 2005 (Wafa News Agency report, 31 December 2005); the Palestinian researcher Salman Abu Sitta's estimate (excluding those in Israel) for 2000 was 8,270,509 (personal communication, 2005.) See also Salman H. Abu Sitta, *The Palestinian Nakba: The Register of Depopulated Localities in Palestine* (London: Palestine Return Centre, 1998).

17. The Hamas victory in the Palestinian Legislative Council elections of January 2006 led to new attempts to revive the PLO's old role.

18. Meron Benvenisti, *Sacred Landscape: the Buried History of the Holy Land Since 1948* (Berkeley: University of California Press, 2000), pp. 11–43.

19. 'Suppression of Jerusalem's Arab and Islamic identity accelerates', *Al-Quds al-Arabi*, 14 January 2005.

20. W. Khalidi, *All That Remains: The Palestinian Villages Occupied and Depopulated by Israel in 1948* (Washington, DC: Institute

for Palestine Studies, 1992); S. Abu Sitta, *Atlas of Palestine* (London: Palestine Land Society, 2005).

21. See review of Hillel Cohen's 2006 book, *Good Arabs* [Hebrew], by Amira Hass in *Haaretz*, 20 September 2006. The book lays out these facts as derived from recently released Israeli security archives.

22. Amongst these may be cited a number in various countries: Diana Allan (ed.), *Voices of the Nakba* (London: Pluto Press, 2021); Ilan Pappe while at Haifa University was engaged with others in an oral history project about the *Nakba* of 1948; Rosemary Sayegh has also worked on oral history taken from Palestinian refugees in the Lebanese camps; May Saykali in the US has worked on an oral history of Haifa, and there are ongoing projects by Mahmoud Issa in Denmark on the history of Lubya, one of the destroyed Palestinian villages of 1948.

23. Ghalia Ali, *Jordan Times*, 30 May 1998; *US Committee for Refugees Country Report: Jordan* (Washington, DC: 22 November 2002).

24. 'Jordan spends about \$1 billion a year on Palestinian refugees', *Jordan News*, 9 May 2022.

25. The Israeli government reportedly set up a committee to assess the claims of Jews who fled Arab countries against those countries. In particular, Israel demanded the restitution of property for the 100,000 Iraqi Jewish refugees, *Jewish Week*, 1 February 2004; Yehouda Shenhav, 'The Jews of Iraq, Zionist ideology, and the property of Palestinian refugees of 1948: an anomaly of accounting', Cambridge University Press online, 29 January 2009: www.cambridge.org/core/journals/international-journal-of-middle-east-studies/article/abs/jews-of-iraq-zionist-ideology-and-the-property-of-the-palestinian-refugees-of-1948-an-anomaly-of-national-accounting/33F43488B8878CD3E766F5E9E0FC2D09

26. A strong Moroccan movement of solidarity with the Palestinians had been in existence for many years, and at various stages in the conflict Moroccans have taken to the streets in mass demonstrations, which the authorities have been unable to

suppress. The largest of these took place during the Second Intifada.

27. Maintaining Israel's 'strategic edge' was a declared US policy. The preferential trade tariff agreement between the US and Israel (signed 9 April 1985), as well as European funding for Israeli research institutions and numerous academic and cultural exchange programmes to the benefit of Israel, were part of the same effort.

3   Israel and the Jews

1.   N.W. Cohen, *American Jews and the Zionist Idea* (Tel Aviv: Ktav Publishing House, 1985).

2.   'Economist tallies swelling cost of Israel to US', *Christian Science Monitor*, 9 December 2002.

3.   'Record $1.1 billion in Israel bonds sold in US in 2016', *Jewish Telegraphic Agency*, 9 February 2017.

4.   Ibid.

5.   Tony Bayfield, 'We need a new kind of Zionism', *Guardian*, 23 March 2005.

6.   US aid to Israel in 1997 alone was estimated at $5.5 billion: see Richard Curtiss, *Washington Report on Middle East Affairs*, December 1997; Jewish National Fund, www.jnf.org; Jeremy M. Sharp, 'US foreign aid to Israel', *Congressional Research Service*, 18 February 2022.

7.   'No one knows the full cost of Israel's settlement ambition', *USA Today*, 14 August 2005.

8.   Scott Wilson, 'Golan Heights Land and lifestyle lure settlers', *Washington Post*, 30 October 2006.

9.   The Israeli National Insurance Institute found that in 2002 32.8 per cent of the population was in poverty, 17.7 per cent of families, and that the percentage of poor children out of a total number of children was rising. After the Netanyahu government was elected in 1997, 1.4 million Israelis were living in poverty and the divide between rich and poor had grown, see 'Finished with Likud, it was poverty not disengagement that determined

the outcome of the Israeli elections', *Al-Ahram Weekly*, 1 April 2006.

10. Nasreen Haddad Haj-Yahya et al., *Statistical Report on Arab Society in Israel: 2021*, 17 March 2022.

11. I. Shahak and N. Mezvinsky, *Jewish Fundamentalism in Israel* (London: Pluto Press, 2000), pp. 96–112.

12. According to the Israeli Central Bureau of Statistics, the proportion of those born in Israel in 1996 was 61.6 per cent. In 1960, it was 37.4 per cent.

13. Ian Lustick, 'Recent trends in emigration from Israel: The impact of Palestinian violence', Paper presented to the annual meeting of the Association for Israel Studies, Jerusalem, 14–16 June 2004; '750,000 Israelis left the Jewish state', *Al-Quds al-Arabi*, 9 December 2003.

14. Noam Arnon, 'It's ours without a majority', *Haaretz*, 28 August 2002; emphasis added.

15. John Rose, *The Myths of Zionism* (London: Pluto Press, 2004), p. 43.

16. Arthur Koestler, *The Thirteenth Tribe: The Khazar Empire and Its Heritage* (London: Hutchinson, 1976); D.M. Dunlop, *The History of the Khazars* (Princeton, NJ: Princeton University Press, 1954); Sand, *The Invention of the Jewish People*.

17. 'Did the Khazars convert to Judaism? New research says "no"', *Science Daily*, 26 June 2014.

18. Isaac Deutscher, *The Non-Jewish Jew and Other Essays* (London: Oxford University Press, 1968), p. 25.

19. Quoted in K. Sabbagh, *Palestine: A Personal History* (London: Atlantic Books, 2005), p. 160.

20. Personal communication with Joachim Martillo, a specialist in the subject, to whom I am indebted for the remarks in this section; see also Deutscher, *Non-Jewish Jew*, p. 96, and 'Racism within the ranks', *Al-Ahram Weekly*, 2–8 September 2004.

21. Cited in Kevin Alan Brook, *The Jews of Khazaria* (Northvale, NJ: Jason Aaronson. 1999), p. 220.

22. Deutscher, *Non-Jewish Jew*, pp. 62, 86–7.

23. 'Haskalah', *Encyclopaedia Judaica* (Jerusalem: Keter Publishing House, 1971), pp. 139–51; 'Assimilation', *Encyclopaedia of*

Judaism (Jerusalem: Jerusalem Publishing House, 2002), pp. 85–7.

24. I. Halevi, *A History of the Jews Ancient and Modern* (London: Zed Books, 1987), pp. 127–34.

25. Rose, *Myths*, p. 102.

26. Deutscher, *Non-Jewish Jew*, pp. 96–7.

27. Michael Novick, *The Holocaust in American Life* (New York: Houghton and Mifflin, 1999), p. 149.

28. Cited in Joseph Massad, 'Deconstructing Holocaust consciousness', *Journal of Palestine Studies*, Vol. 32, No. 1 (2002), pp. 78–89.

29. Akiva Orr, *The Un-Jewish State: The Politics of Jewish Identity in Israel* (London: Ithaca Press, 1983).

30. 'Anti-Zionism is anti-Semitism', *Guardian*, 29 November 2003.

31. Rebecca Gould, 'The IHRA definition of antisemitism', *The Political Quarterly*, Vol. 91 (2020), pp. 825–31.

32. Areeb Ullah, 'Antisemitism: what is the IHRA definition and why is it controversial?', *Middle East Eye*, 16 April 2021.

33. Gould, 'The IHRA definition of antisemitism'.

34. Jacob Magid, 'Israeli envoy to UN "expects" Guterres to adopt the IHRA definition of antisemitism', *Times of Israel*, 26 January 2022.

4   The Israeli-Palestinian 'Peace Process'

1. For much of the material in this section, I am indebted to Charles Smith's excellent book, *Palestine and the Arab-Israeli Conflict* (Basingstoke: Macmillan Education, 1994), and to William Quandt's *Decade of Decisions: American Policy Towards the Arab-Israeli Conflict, 1967–1976* (Berkeley: University of California Press, 1978).

2. For example, no lawyers were present in the Palestinian negotiating team at Oslo and no maps were used to agree to Israel's division of the territories into areas A, B and C after the Oslo 2 Agreement.

3. 'The Sharm al-Shaykh Memorandum (Wye II) and related documents', *Journal of Palestine Studies*, Vol. 29 (2000), pp. 143–56.

5 The One-State Solution

1. 'Our future in 2020', *Nativ*, May 2005. Report by Zuhair Andrawus, *Al-Quds al-Arabi*, 23 May 2005.
2. Interview with Ari Shavit, *Haaretz*, 4 April 2006.
3. Shlaim, *The Iron Wall*, pp. 12–14.
4. Amir Oren, 'Living by the sword, for all time', *Haaretz*, 2 May 2006.
5. Zack Beauchamp, 'How does the world feel about Israel/Palestine?', *Vox.com*, 14 May 2018 www.vox.com/2018/11/20/18080086/israel-palestine-global-opinion.
6. 'Internal Biden memo said to back the two-state solution along 1967 lines', *Times of Israel*, 17 March 2021.
7. The Palestinian film maker, Leila Sansour, is one of these (personal communication).
8. Ilan Pappe, *A History of Modern Palestine: One Land, Two Peoples* (Cambridge: Cambridge University Press, 2004), pp. 86–7.
9. Henry Cattan, *Palestine and International Law: The Legal Aspects of the Arab-Israeli Conflict* (London: Longman, 1973), pp. 42–56.
10. Muhammad Muslih, 'Towards an analysis of the resolutions of the Palestine National Council', *Journal of Palestine Studies*, Vol. 19, No. 4 (1999), pp. 3–29. This article contains a detailed analysis of the formal Palestinian position on the two-state solution.
11. 'Obama seeks to pave the way to Mideast deal after he leaves office', *New York Times*, 8 March 2016.
12. 'What to know about Trump's Middle East plan', *New York Times*, 29 January 2020.
13. *Report of the Special Rapporteur on the situation of human rights in the Palestinian territories occupied by Israel since 1967*, UN Doc. E/CN.4/2006/29, 17 January 2006.

Notes

14. An excellent summary of these logistical problems is provided by the PLO Negotiations Affairs Department study, *Israelis' Pre-Emption of a Viable Two-State Solution* (Ramallah, 2002); see also, 'Israel redraws the roadmap, building quietly and quickly', *Guardian*, 18 October 2005, and 'Is this the end for a Palestinian state?', *Guardian*, 4 March 2003.

15. Jeff Halper, *Obstacles to Peace: A Reframing of the Palestinian–Israeli Conflict*, Palestinian Mapping Project, 2004, pp. 8–18; 'A Palestinian prison state?', *Boston Globe*, 11 April 2005.

16. Jan de Jong, 'The end of the two-state solution – a geo-political analysis', in Mahdi Abdul Hadi (ed.), *Palestinian–Israeli Impasse: Exploring Alternative Solutions to the Palestine–Israel Conflict* (Jerusalem: PASSIA, 2005), pp. 315–41.

17. Michael Tarazi, 'Two peoples, one state', *New York Times*, 5 October 2004.

18. Ali Jarbawi, 'Remaining Palestinian options', *The Arab World Geographer*, Vol. 8, No 3 (2005).

19. Ari Shavit, 'Cry the beloved two-state solution', *Haaretz*, 8 August 2003. I will have recourse to cite this excellent article several times in what follows.

20. Ghada Karmi, 'Reconciliation in the Arab-Israeli conflict', *Mediterranean Politics*, Vol. 4, No. 3 (1999), pp. 104–14. The survey results are unpublished.

21. The Ramallah-based Near East Counselling Institution found that 71 per cent of West Bank refugees were living in extreme poverty: 20 November 2006, https://imemc.org/article/22759/

22. This is the Palestinian academic, Sari Nusseibeh's view: 'Pushing Mideast peace', *New York Times*, 1 November 2003.

23. Effi Eitam, a former Israeli minister with explicitly racist views, provoked a storm of controversy when he talked of the need to expel 'the Arabs': 'Calls for "removal" of Arabs', *Jerusalem Post*, 14 September 2006.

24. Jeffrey Heller, 'About half of Israeli Jews want to expel Arabs, survey finds', *Reuters*, 8 March 2016 www.reuters.com/article/us-israel-palestinians-survey-idUSKCN0WA1HI

25. Human Rights Watch, *A Threshold Crossed*, 27 April 2021, www.hrw.org/report/2021/04/27/threshold-crossed/israeli-authorities-and-crimes-apartheid-and-persecution

26. William Brinner and Moses Rischin (eds), *The Life and Times of Judah L. Magnes* (Albany: State University of New York Press, 1987); Arthur Goren, *Dissenter in Zion: From the Writings of Judah L. Magnes* (Cambridge, MA: Harvard University Press, 1982), pp. 307–67.

27. J.L. Magnes et al., *Palestine – United or Divided? The Case for a Bi-National Palestine Before the United Nations* (Westport, CT: Greenwood Press, 1947, reprinted 1983); M. Buber, J.L. Magnes, E. Simon (eds), *Towards Union in Palestine: Essays on Zionism and Jewish-Arab Cooperation* (Jerusalem: Ihud, 1947).

28. Noam Chomsky, *Middle East Illusions* (Lanham, MD: Rowman and Littlefield, 2003), p. 67.

29. Susan Lee-Hattis, *The Binational Idea in Palestine During Mandatory Times* (Haifa: Shikmona, 1970).

30. Meron Benvenisti, 'The binational question', *Haaretz*, 7 November 2002.

31. As'ad Ghanem, 'The binational solution: Conceptual background and contemporary debate', in Abdul Hadi (ed.), *Palestinian–Israeli Impasse*, p. 36.

32. Shavit, 'Cry the beloved two-state solution'; Meron Benvenisti, 'The binational option', *Haaretz*, 7 November 2002; Idem, *Intimate Enemies: Jews and Arabs in a shared land* (Berkeley: University of California Press, 1995), pp. 31ff; Edward Said, 'The one-state solution', *New York Times*, 10 January 1999; Azmi Bishara, *New Realties, Old Problems* (London: Pluto Press, 1998), pp. 212–26.

33. Interview with Edward Said, 'My right to return', Ari Shavit, *Haaretz Magazine*, 10 August 2000.

34. Dom Peretz, 'A binational approach to the Palestine conflict', *Law and Contemporary Problems*, Vol. 33, No. 1 (1968), pp. 31–43.

35. Daniel Elazar, *Two Peoples—One Land* (Lanham, MD: University Press of America, 1991), pp. 180–85.

36. 'Justice for Palestine? Q and A on prospects for a solution', *Znet*, 30 March 2003; Chomsky, *Middle East Illusions*, pp. 39–71.

Notes

37. Mark Heller and Sari Nusseibeh, *No Trumpets, No Drums: A two state settlement of the Israeli–Palestinian conflict* (London: I.B. Tauris, 1991).

38. Mathias Mossberg, 'Superimposing a solution', *Foreign Policy*, 27 June 2006; Deb Reich, 'Beyond the onion of blame', *Counterpunch*, 30 October 2002.

39. Lama Abu-Odeh, 'The case for binationalism', *Boston Review*, 14 March 2005; Tarif Abboushi, 'New road map: one state, modelled after US', *Houston Chronicle*, 11 June 2003.

40. Nasser Abufarha, 'Alternative Palestinian agenda – proposal for an alternative configuration in Palestine-Israel', in Abdul Hadi (ed.), *Palestinian–Israeli Impasse*, pp. 145–87.

41. Andrew Reding, 'Call it "Israel-Palestine" – try federal solution in Middle East', *Pacific News Service*, 26 June 2002.

42. Issam Nashashibi, 'Back to the future: is there a more equitable Palestinian-Israeli solution in UNSCOP's "Minority Plan"?' *Washington Report on Middle East Affairs*, January–February 1999.

43. Israel Shamir, 'The Malaysian solution', www.unz.com/ishamir/the-malaysian-solution/, 25 January 2003.

44. Elazar, *Two Peoples*.

45. Tamar Hermann, 'The bi-national idea in Israel/Palestine: past and present', *Nations and Nationalism*, Vol. 11, No. 3 (2005), pp. 381–401.

46. M. Muslih, 'Towards co-existence: an analysis of the Resolutions of the Palestine National Council', *Journal of Palestine Studies*, Vol. 19, No. 4 (1990), pp. 13–16.

47. William Quandt, Fuad Jabber and Ann Mosley Lesch, *The Politics of Palestinian Nationalism* (Berkeley: University of California Press, 1973), p. 144.

48. Alain Gresh, *The PLO: The Struggle Within – Towards an Independent Palestinian State* (London: Zed Books, 1983), pp. 7–50.

49. Article 6 of the Palestine National Charter as amended in 1964, stipulated this.

50. Yehoshafat Harkabi, *Fedayeen Action and Arab Strategy*, Adelphi Papers, No. 53 (London: Institute for Strategic Studies, 1968).

One State

51. Quandt et al., *Politics*, pp. 100–12.

52. Reported by *Newsweek*, 27 April 1970 (cited in Quandt, *Politics*, p. 105).

53. Gresh, *The PLO*, p. 50.

54. Fouzi el-Asmar, Uri Davis and Naim Khader, *Towards a Socialist Republic of Palestine* (London: Ithaca Press, 1978).

55. 'Palestinians ready to push for one state', *Associated Press*, 9 January 2004.

56. Gary Sussman, 'The challenge to the two-state solution', *MERIP*, Report 231, March 2005.

57. Effi Eitam, 'No sovereignty for Arabs in Eretz Israel', *Haaretz*, 8 April 2002.

58. For example, Tikva Honig-Parnass, 'Bi-nationalism versus secular-democratic state', *News from Within*, 13 March 2002, and July 2002, 'A secular–democratic state', interview with Eli Aminov; Ghada Karmi, 'One land two peoples', *Haaretz*, 9 July 2002; 'A secular democratic state in historic Palestine: an idea whose time has come' (in Arabic), *Al-Adab*, July 2002; 'The right of return and the unitary state in Israel/Palestine', *Race Traitor*, No. 16, Winter 2005.

59. Helena Cobban, 'A binational Israel-Palestine', *Christian Science Monitor*, 9 October 2003.

60. Jeff Halper, 'Preparing for a post-Road Map struggle against apartheid', Paper given to the UN International Conference on Civil Society in Support of the Palestinian People, New York, 5 September 2003.

61. Daniel Gavron, *The Other Side of Despair: Jews and Arabs in the Promised Land* (Lanham, MD: Rowman and Littlefield, 2003); Peter Hirschberg, 'One-state awakening', *Haaretz*, 12 December 2003.

62. Daniel Lazare, 'The one-state solution', *Nation*, 11 October 2004.

63. Daniel Lazare, 'The one-state solution: However utopian, binationalism may be the last hope for Israeli-Palestinian peace', book review, *Nation*, December 2003.

64. Tony Judt, 'Israel: The alternative', *New York Review of Books*, Vol. 50, No. 16, 23 October 2003.

182

Notes

65. Nathaniel Popper, 'Embattled academic Tony Judt defends call for binational state', *Forward*, 26 December 2003.

66. 'Orthodox Jews protest elections held in the Zionist state of Israel', www.nkusa.org/activities/demonstrations/2006Mar28 Jerusalem.cfm, 28 March 2006.

67. www.nkusa.org, 8 November 2006.

68. Financial support for this association was rumoured to have come from Libya, which antagonised many potential members.

69. Mortaza Sahibzada, convenor of the London One-State group, www.one-state.org, last accessed in January 2005. Also see the list of one-state groups in Abdul Hadi (ed.), *Palestinian-Israeli Impasse*, pp. 341–2.

70. Virginia Tilley, *The One-State Solution* (Ann Arbor, MI: University of Michigan Press, 2005); idem, 'The one-state solution', *London Review of Books*, Vol. 25, No. 21, 6 November 2003.

71. gp/org/israel_palestine, 7 July 2020.

72. The London one-state group website, www.one-state.org, had a comprehensive archive of single-state articles.

73. 'Rafsanjani proposes uniting Israel, Palestine under one government', *Jordan Times*, 14 November 2004.

74. *Isratine*, Gaddafi Official Website, 8 May 2003.

75. 'Gaddafi walks out, boycotts Arab summit', *Reuters*, 22 May 2004.

76. The Peace Index, October 2003, Tami Steinmetz Centre for Peace Research, Tel Aviv University, http://spirit.tau.ac.il/peace index/2003; 'Peace Index – demographic fears favour unilateral separation', *Haaretz*, 7 December 2003.

77. Jerusalem Media and Communication Centre, 'Palestinians in the West Bank favour one binational state over the two-state solution', October 2021.

78. Magnes et al., *Palestine – United or Divided?*.

79. Salim Tamari, 'The dubious lure of binationalism', in Abdul Hadi (ed.), *Palestinian–Israeli Impasse*, pp. 67–73.

80. Halper, 'A Middle Eastern confederation: a regional "two-stage" approach to the Israeli-Palestinian conflict', *Arab Media Internet Network*, 15 December 2002.

81. Posted on John Whitbeck's website, 7 October 2004 (no longer available).

82. Uri Avnery, 'A binational state? God forbid!', *Journal of Palestine Studies*, Vol. 28, No. 4 (1999), pp. 55–60.

83. 'Abed Rabbo rules out bi-national state', Palestine Media Centre official website, January 2004.

84. 'New Fatah chief al-Qaddumi goal is to eliminate Israel in "second stage"', *Middle East Newsline*, 23 December 2004.

85. Nancy Crawshaw, *The Cyprus Revolution: An Account of the Struggle for Union with Greece* (London: Allen and Unwin, 1978), pp. 364–97.

86. William Dalrymple, 'The final place of refuge for Christians in the Middle East', *Guardian*, 2 September 2006.

87. The Palestinian political scientist As'ad Ghanem disagreed with such notions. His view was that the ethnic nature of the Jewish and Palestinian national movements was too strong to permit the development of a common civil identity, in Abdul Hadi (ed.), *Palestinian–Israeli Impasse*, p. 59).

88. Yoav Peled, 'Zionist realities', *New Left Review*, Vol. 38, March–April 2006, pp. 21–36, and Virginia Tilley's reply to it, 'The secular solution', pp. 37–57.

89. Avraham Burg, 'End of an era', *Haaretz*, 5 August 2005.

90. Mouna Younis, *Liberation and Democratisation: The South African and Palestinian National Movements* (Minneapolis: University of Minnesota Press, 2000), pp. 1–21.

91. 'Brothers in arms – Israel's secret pact with Pretoria', *Guardian*, 7 February 2006.

92. 'Worlds apart', *Guardian*, 6 February 2006.

93. 'A one-state solution for Israel/Palestine: inevitable or pie in the sky?' *Media Review Network*, 2 March 2004.

94. *Truth and Reconciliation Commission of South Africa Report*, official website, 21 March 2003.

95. Abd al-Alim Muhammad, *The Future of the Arab-Israeli Conflict: The Palestinian Unitary Democratic State* (Cairo: Centre of Political and Strategic Studies Publications, 1999), p. 59.

96. 'Israeli practices towards the Palestinian people and the question of apartheid', UN Economic and Social Commission for Western Asia, ESQWA, 64 pp., Beirut, 2017.

97. 'This is apartheid: a regime of Jewish supremacy from the Jordan river to the Mediterranean sea', B'tselem, 12 January 2021.

98. 'A threshold crossed: Israeli authorities and the crimes of apartheid and persecution', Human Rights Watch, 27 April 2021.

99. Amnesty International, 'Israel's apartheid against Palestinians: A cruel system of domination and a crime against humanity', 1 February 2022.

100. Peter Beaumont, 'Abandoning the two-state solution is "no joke", Palestine officials say', *Guardian*, 15 February 2017.

6 Eleven Days in May

1. The following account of events in those eleven days has been put together from a variety of press and media sources and eyewitness reports, which I have not detailed here.

2. 'Israeli president warns of civil war as Jews, Arabs clash over Gaza', Reuters, 12 May 2021.

3. 'How Hamas's arsenal shaped the Gaza war of May 2021', *Forbes*, 25 May 2021.

4. Sebastien Roblin, 'Israel's bombardment of Gaza: methods, weapons, and impact', *Forbes*, 26 May 2021.

5. 'What do Black Lives Matter and Palestine solidarity have in common?' *OpenDemocracy*, 25 May 2021.

6. 'Why Black Lives Matter is backing the Palestinian cause', *Times*, 31 May 2021.

7. *Forbes*, 26 May 2021.

8. Diana Buttu, 'The myth of coexistence in Israel', *New York Times*, 25 May 2021.

9. Bethany McKernan and Sufian Taha, '"It's going to explode": Young Palestinians look to the gun amid Israeli offensive', *Guardian*, 21 September 2022.

10. Zena al-Tahhan, 'The occupied West Bank cities at centre of resistance to Israel', *Aljazeera*, 13 September 2022.
11. Fatima Abdul Karim, 'Unrest turns deadly in West Bank as PA's grip loosens', *Wall Street Journal*, 20 September 2022.
12. Zena al-Tahhan, 'Palestinians strike against Israeli siege on Jerusalem camp', *Aljazeera*, 12 October 2022.
13. 'Palestine: hundreds of Palestinians confront Israeli forces in East Jerusalem', *Middle East Eye*, 13 October 2022.

Conclusion: The Future

1. Yehoshafat Harkabi, *Israel's Fateful Decisions* (London: I.B. Tauris, 1988), p. 209.
2. 'Trump releases Mideast plan that strongly favors Israel', *New York Times*, 28 January 2020.
3. 'Israel has shown its capability for military retaliation, but it is no solution for two million hungry Palestinians', *Yediot Ahronot*, 6 September 2006.
4. 'Time to break the silence on Palestine', *New York Times*, 19 January 2019.
5. Zuhair Andrawus, in *Al-Quds al-Arabi*, 1 September 2006.
6. Ari Shavit, 'Cry the beloved two state solution', *Haaretz*, 8 August 2003.
7. Ibid.
8. Ibid.

Index

n refers to a note

Abbas, Mahmoud 167
Abboushi, Tarif 110
Abraham Accords (2020) 3
Abu-Odeh, Lama 110
Abufarha, Nasser 111
Ahmadinejad, Mahmoud 138
Al-Aqsa Mosque 151–2, 158
al-Masri, Munib 89
al-Quds al-Arabi 97
al-Sai'qa (organisation) 116
Alami, Musa 105–6
Alawite 135
Aljazeera 158
American Israel Public Affairs
    Committee (AIPAC) 35
Amish 40
Amnesty International 144
Anglo-American Committee of
    Inquiry (1946) 104, 126
Anti-Defamation League 158
anti-semitism: equating with
    criticism of Israel 4, 13, 35,
    40, 46, 51–2, 146, 166
Arab Human Development
    Report (2002) 20
Arab League Summit (Tunis,
    2004) 123
Arab Liberation Front 116
Arab Peace Initiative (2002) 15

Arab states
    impact of establishment of
        Israel on 19–28
    militarisation of 20–1
    normalisation of relations with
        Israel 3, 15, 22, 29–30, 100
    response to establishment of
        Israel 2–3, 29–33
Arab-Israeli Wars *see* Six-Day
        War; Yom Kippur War
Arafat, Yasser 27, 61, 62–6, 71–2,
        93, 114, 117
Association for One Democratic
        State in Palestine-Israel 121,
        125, 183*n*68
Atwan, Abdel Bari 98
Avnery, Uri 131–2, 133–4

B'Tselem (organisation) 144
Bahrain 3, 15, 22, 100
Balfour, Arthur 12
Balfour Declaration (1917) 14,
        44, 171–2*n*5
Barak, Ehud 66, 67
Barghouti, Marwan 118
BBC opinion poll (2012) 84
Begin, Menachem 108
Beinart, Peter 146, 158
Beirut: siege of (1982) 31

Belgium federation 111–2
Ben-Gurion, David 10, 21, 26–7, 28, 49, 104
Benvenisti, Meron 108, 169
Bharatiya Janata Party (BJP) 23
bi-nationalism 103–13, 119, 126–7, 133–4
Biden, Joe 86, 157
Birthright Israel (organisation) 48
Bishara, Azmi 108
Black Lives Matter (BLM) 83, 156–7
Blinken, Anthony 157
Boycott, Divestment and Sanctions (BDS) 4, 5
Brit Shalom (organisation) 26, 104
British Mandate 26, 89, 91, 105, 161–2
Buber, Martin 26, 107
Bund Party 46
Burg, Avraham 137–8
Bush, George H.W. 60, 69
Bush, George W. 69, 92

Camp David Accords (1979) 58, 109
Camp David Summit (2000) 66–70
Canada federation 111
Carter, Jimmy 57–8
Chomsky, Noam 109
Churchill White Paper (1922) 44–5
Clinton, Bill 66–7
Cobban, Helena 119

Confederation of Presidents of Jewish Organisations 35
Corbyn, Jeremy 51, 83
Covid-19 pandemic 36
Cyprus conflict (1974) 107, 134

Dayan, Moshe 11–12

Egypt 20, 22, 29, 58, 100
Eiland, Giora 79
Eitam, Effi 119, 179n23
Emile Touma Institute 122
Erekat, Saeb 150
Eritrea 23
Ethiopia 22–3
European Union 2, 87

Facebook 156
Fahd Plan (1981) 58–9
Faris, Qaddura 118
Fatah Party 116, 118
Fez Plan (1982) 90
Filastin al-Jadida (New Palestine) 106
Floyd, George 156–7
French Revolution 45
Frisch, Hillel 137

Gaddafi, Muammar 123
Gallup World Affairs Survey 84
Gantz, Benny 153
Gavron, Daniel 119–20
Gaza 3–4, 58, 61, 78, 93, 107, 145, 162
    assaults on 13, 53, 81–2, 83–4, 85, 130, 154–6
Geneva Convention (4th) 145

Index

Germany: Nazi era 46, 47
Golan Heights 36
Goldstein, Baruch 37
Green Line 144, 154
Green Party (US) 122
Group of 77 countries 86
Gulf War (1990–91) 60, 61

Haaretz 9, 38, 78, 82, 148, 167
Halper, Jeff 93–4, 119–20, 130
   Decolonising Israel 128
Hamas 24–5, 62, 82, 97, 154–6,
   158, 165
Hammami, Said 92
Hanegbi, Haim 94–5, 108, 169
Hashomer Hatzair (organisation)
   104
Hebron 37, 64, 67
Hermann, Tamar 112–3
Holocaust, the 13, 35, 46–7
Horn of Africa 23
Human Rights Watch 100, 144
Hussein, King of Jordan 59, 108
Hussein, Saddam 61, 134–5
Husseini, Fawzi 106

Ihud Party 104, 126
India 23–4
International Criminal Court
   86, 149
International Holocaust Remem-
   brance Alliance (IHRA)
   51–2
International Olympic
   Committee 86
Intifada
   1st (1987) 13, 24, 61–2, 90, 164

   2nd (2000) 13, 25, 36–7, 51,
     68–9, 120–1
Iran 22, 123
Iraq 22, 29, 33, 135
   US invasion of 23, 32, 60, 135
Islamic groups 24–5, 62, 82, 155
Israel
   creation of 1–2
   emigration from 37–8, 167
   as a Jewish state 8, 27, 38
   population of 144
   poverty in 175–6n9
   Western support for 3, 20,
     47–8, 74–5
   for other topics relating to
     Israel/Palestine, *see* the
     topic, e.g. Six-Day War;
     United States
Israeli Committee Against House
   Demolition (ICAHD) 93–4
Israeli Defence Forces (IDF) 83,
   155
Israeli Law of Return (1950) 49

Jabotinsky, Ze'ev 'The Iron
   Wall' 11, 81
Jenin 159
Jerusalem 73, 93–4, 59–60, 112
Jerusalem Media and Communi-
   cation Centre 123–4
Jewish Currents 146
Jewish dialects 45
Jewish jokes 41–2
Jewish Week 121
'Jewishness' 43–4, 48–9
Jews
   American Jews 34–5

Ashkenazi Jews 40, 41–2, 49
assimilation in Europe of 45–6
cultural Jews 49
as an ethnic group 39–43
European Jews 38–42, 47–9
German Orthodox Jews 47
identification with Israel by
    34–8, 47–50
Israeli Jews 36–7, 51, 100
Lithuanian Jews 39
Neturei Karta Jews 121
Orthodox Jews 40–1, 44
Polish Jews 39
Reform Jews 47
religious Jews 37, 40
Sabra Jews 37
Satmar Jews 121
secular Jews 48
Jordan 3, 20, 21, 22, 31, 79–80,
    90, 100
'Black September' (1970–71)
    114
Jordan Valley 67, 93
Jordan-West Bank confederation
    59, 79–80, 90, 108–9, 114,
    164
Judt, Tony 120

Karmi, Ghada *Married to Another
    Man* 1, 127
Keeley, Robert 131
Kerry, John 92
Khalidi, Ahmed 105
Khalidi, Walid 28
Khazar hypothesis 39, 44
Khomeini, Ayatollah 138
Koestler, Arthur 39

Kovel, Joel *Overcoming Zionism*
    127
Kurds 22, 107
Kuwait 29, 32

Labour Party (UK) 51, 83
Lazare, Daniel 120
League for Jewish-Arab
    Rapprochement and
    Co-operation 106
League of Arab States 85, 87
League of Nations 89
Lebanon 20, 21–2, 30–1, 57, 167
Lehava (organisation) 152
Levy, Gideon 78, 148
Linur, Irit 167–8
London School of Economics 85
Lughod, Ibrahim Abu 129–30

Madrid Conference (1991) 60–1
Magnes, Judah 26, 104, 107, 126
Malaysia federation 112
Mandela, Nelson 147
Mapai Party 104
Mauritania 22
Mediation and Conflict
    Management Centre 124
Mitchell, Senator George 69
Morocco 15, 22, 30, 32, 100,
    174–5n26
Morris, Benny 9–11, 81
Mossberg, Mathias 109–10
Movement for Jewish Reform 35
Movement for One Secular State
    121
Muhammad bin Sultan, Crown
    Prince of Saudi Arabia 22

Index

Munich Declaration (2012) 125
Muslim Brotherhood 24

Nablus 159
Nakba (1948) 27, 82, 96, 174*n*22
Nasser, Gamal Abdel 14
New York Times 146, 158
non-sectarian states 113–7
Novick, Michael 47
Nusseibeh, Sari 109

Obama, Barack 92
Ocasio-Cortez, Alexandria 156
Omar, Ilhan 156
One Democratic State
    Foundation 124–5
One Democratic State Group
    (ODS) 121, 125
one-state solution 5–6, 99–103,
    108, 122–33
  literature on 125–9
  obstacles to 136–40
  secular democratic one-state
    113–25, 134–6
Operation Cast Lead (2008–9)
    83–4
Operation Protective Edge
    (2014) 83, 84
Oren, Amir 82
Organisation of Islamic
    Cooperation 85
Orr, Akiva 48
Oslo Accords (1993) 25, 27, 36,
    55, 62–5, 68, 71–2, 88–9,
    92–3, 108, 115, 145, 149

Palestine
  partition of 59, 89–91, 161–2
  international support for 3–4,
    83–4, 156–8
  UN recognition of 85–6, 149
Palestine Islamic Foundation 24
Palestine Liberation Organisa-
    tion (PLO) 3, 24, 27, 57, 59,
    82, 90–1, 97
  and Oslo Accords 60–6
  rejection of Resolution 242 by
    56
  and secular democratic state
    113–7
Palestine-Israel Pulse 124
Palestinian Authority (PA) 65,
    67, 69, 82, 94, 145–6, 150 167
Palestinian Center for Policy and
    Survey Research 123–4
Palestinian Movement 115, 117
Palestinian National Charter
    (1964) 90, 115
Palestinian National Council
    (PNC) 59, 90, 91, 115
Palestinian refugees 30–2, 67,
    97–9
Palestinian uprising (2021) 53,
    151–60
Palestinians
  equal rights for 147–8, 150
  population of 173*n*16
Palin Commission (1920) 40
Pappé, Ilan 122
Passover 43
Peace to Prosperity Plan (2020)
    70, 164
Peel Commission (1937) 89
Peretz, Dom 108
Pew Research Center 84, 100

Popular Democratic Front for the Liberation of Palestine (PDFLP) 114, 116
Popular Front for the Liberation of Palestine (PFLP) 114
Punjabi Sikhs 40

Qaddumi, Farouk 132
Qatar 22
Quartet on the Middle East 69–70, 86
Qumsiyeh, Mazin *Sharing the Land of Canaan* 128
Qurei, Ahmed 94, 118

Rabbis for Peace 121
Rabbo, Yasir Abed 132
Rabin, Yitzhak 35–6, 61–2
Rafsanjani, Hashemi 122–3
Ramadan 152
Reagan, Ronald 59
Reiner, Markus 126
Right of Return 30, 98, 117
Right to Return Coalition 121
Road Map for Peace 69–70, 92
Rogers Plan (1969) 114
Ruppin, Arthur 26
Russia: invasion of Ukraine by 2
Russian Revolution 45

Sadat, Anwar 65
Safieh, Afif 129
Said, Edward 108
Samuel, Herbert, 1st Viscount 26
Saudi Peace Plan *see* Arab Peace Initiative
Saudi Arabia 22, 58

School of Oriental and African Studies (SOAS) 85, 124
settlements 36–7, 67, 78
Shalom, Silvan 22
shared state 1, 26–7
Sharm al-Sheikh Memorandum (1999) 66–7
Sharon, Ariel 69, 79, 164
Sheikh Jarrah 151–3
Shu'fat refugee camp 160
Simon, Ernest 126
Sitta, Salman Abu 28
Six-Day War (1967) 34, 47, 144
Smilansky, Moshe 126
social media: support for Palestine in 156
South Africa 119, 139, 147
    Truth and Reconciliation Commission 139–40
Sudan 15, 22, 30, 100
suicide bombings 25
Sussman, Gary 118
Swiss federation 111
Syria 3, 20, 29, 33, 135

Tamari, Salim 130
Tay-Sachs disease 41
Tilley, Virginia 122, 135–6
    The One-State Solution 127
Tisha B'Av festival 43
Tlaib, Rashida 156
Trump, Donald 31, 70, 92, 164
Tunisia 22
Turkey 22–3, 172n6
two-state solution 17–18, 86–97, 98–9, 101, 109, 149–50, 162–3

Index

Ukraine: Russian invasion of 2
United Nations
  Resolution 181 (1947) 27, 59, 89, 91
  Resolution 242 (1967) 55–8, 64, 86, 114
  Resolution 338 (1973) 91
UN Partition Plan (1947) 27
UN Relief and Works Agency for Refugees (UNRWA) 31, 160
UN Special Committee on Palestine (UNSCOP) 112, 126
UN Special Rapporteur 93
UNESCO 86, 149
United Arab Emirates (UAE) 3, 15, 22, 100
United Jewish Israel Appeal 'Our Future in 2020' 79
United States
  civil rights movement 147–8
  support for Israel by 2, 35, 57, 72, 138, 157, 175n6, 175n27
  support for Palestine in 3, 156–7

universities: support for Palestine 84–6
University and College Union (UCU) 85
university students: support for Palestine 84–5

Weizmann, Chaim 48, 104, 107
West Bank 53, 59, 67, 74, 78, 79–80, 93, 107, 145
Wiesel, Elie 47
World Bank 21, 145

Yediot Ahronot 118
Yemen 29
'Yiddishism' 41
Yom Kippur War (1973) 21, 29, 47, 109, 114

Zionism 8–18, 34–5, 46, 81, 99, 168–9
  Christian Zionists 13, 138
  cultural Zionism 104, 137
  political Zionism 41, 42, 48, 138

The Pluto Press Newsletter

Hello friend of Pluto!

Want to stay on top of the best radical books we publish?

Then sign up to be the first to hear about our new books, as well as special events, podcasts and videos.

You'll also get 50% off your first order with us when you sign up.

Come and join us!

Go to bit.ly/PlutoNewsletter

Thanks to our Patreon subscriber:

Ciaran Kane

Who has shown generosity and comradeship in support of our publishing.

Check out the other perks you get by subscribing to our Patreon – visit patreon.com/plutopress.

Subscriptions start from £3 a month.